popular music:

popular music:
the age of multimedia

Andrew Blake

Middlesex
University
PRESS

First published in 2007 by Middlesex University Press

Copyright © Andrew Blake

ISBN-10: 1 904750 20 6

ISBN-13: 978 1 904750 20 8

A CIP catalogue record for this book is available from The British Library

Design by Helen Taylor

Printed in the UK by Cambridge Printing

Middlesex University Press
North London Business Park
Oakleigh Road South
London N11 1QS

Tel: +44 (0)20 8411 4162
Fax: +44 (0)20 8411 4167

www.mupress.co.uk

Contents

Foreword and acknowledgements

This book explores the problems and possibilities in the relationship between music and digital technologies and cultures in the early twenty-first century. Though my own opinions will probably be easy to discern, it's not my principal intention here to argue for or against any particular settlement of the controversies surrounding the making, distribution, ownership and uses of music.

The time for research for this book, and for the opportunity to write the book itself, were supported during 2005–6 firstly by the University of Winchester, and then by the splendid research leave scheme administered by the Arts and Humanities Research Council. I am most grateful to each. Thanks also to Clive Bloom, the editor of this series, for commissioning the book and the editorial staff at Middlesex University Press who have helped to see it through to publication.

My grateful thanks go to the interviewees who gave their time, for email discussion or for group or telephone interviews, to help in the research process. These included people representing among other organisations EMI, LogicaCMG, the British Phonograph Industry, the BBC, the Department for Culture, Media and Sport, and the Department for Trade and Industry. I also thank everyone else I have talked with, individually or in groups, about the ways in which they use music and/or would like to use music via computers, mobile phones and other electronic devices.

Individual interviewees and group members are not otherwise named or identified, and took part in interviews and discussions on that basis. However, I would like specifically to thank friends, research students and academic colleagues who have contributed to the development of my ideas – particular thanks go to Inga Bryden, Jeremy Gilbert, Rupa Huq, Jim Ingham, Graham Jeffery, Fran Mason, George McKay, Stephen Hill, Iain MacRury, and Stevie Simkin. I have already talked and written about some of the issues discussed here. Thanks to staff and students from Kingston University, Southampton University, the University of Winchester, the University of Westminster and the University of East London, who have patiently heard various versions of the chapters and who have helped in the book's development. Finally, in preparing associated work for publication my thoughts have also benefited greatly from the editorial input of Nicholas Cook, Kasia Wieckowska, Jopi Nyman, Paul Manning and Amanda Bayley.

Introduction

'It is the iPod generation – kids don't want to listen to just one genre of music any more.'

Dawn McKay, co-founder of Ibiza club Manumission, August 2006[1]

Music of all genres has never seemed so ubiquitous, and above all so personal, as it does in the age of the iPod and the multimedia mobile phone. And the iPod itself really did seem ubiquitous in the summer of 2006; so ubiquitous that it was no longer in any sense 'cool'. Docking stations for iPods were being built into the sailors' quarters in new Royal Navy ships. At the World Cup held in Germany, the trademark white earphones of Apple's device were seen adorning footballers as they descended from their team coaches to enter the arena. Meanwhile UK Deputy Prime Minister John Prescott, who was relieved of his official country residence after a number of personal scandals, reflected that the thing he would miss most would be walking round the garden in the company of his iPod.

But as well as pleasing the ears of its user, this convenient little device could also have a more sinister significance. Responding to a reported upsurge in street robberies in London, a communications officer from London police headquarters Scotland Yard said that the rise in muggings was down to growing numbers of young people carrying mobile phones, iPods and other personal music players: young people were stealing other young people's status symbols, and their music.

And then there was this little sign of the times. Harraj Mann was on his way to Durham airport. He noticed that the taxi's music system would allow him to plug in his iPod, and he played some classic British pop songs, each of which he endorsed to the taxi driver with his own enthusiasm. But the lyrics of these well-known songs produced an extraordinary response from the driver. Hearing phrases such as 'The war is declared, let the battle come down' (from the Clash's 'London Calling') and 'The hammer of the gods will drive our ship to new lands, to fight the horde' (from Led Zeppelin's 'Immigrant Song'), the suspicious driver alerted the police. The unfortunate Mr Mann was

---

[1] Mark Brown, 'On the Island of Dance, Rave gives way for Rock', www.guardian.co.uk, 14 August 2006, accessed 14 August 2006

frogmarched off his flight by Durham police and detained under the Terrorism Act. By the time it was established that he did not pose a security risk – he was released without charge – his plane had taken off.

Harraj Mann's unpleasant adventure is entirely characteristic of the cultural paranoia of the early twenty-first century. A few months later a number of young British citizens, all of the Muslim faith, were arrested on suspicion of plotting to blow up as many as twelve passenger aircraft, in flight. It was reported that their plan was to blow up passenger jets with liquid explosives hidden in hand luggage that would be combined on board with a detonating device, possibly hidden in an iPod. Reporting journalists noted that mobile phones had been used to trigger the bombs used in an attack on the Madrid railway system in 2004. For a few days, as a result of these suspicions, iPods, mobile phones, portable games players, laptops and other hi tech computing and communications devices were banned from passenger hand luggage. Passengers responded with horror to these new regulations, expressing sorrow at the temporary loss of their cherished music players, and fears that the separation might be permanent. They claimed that the players, phones and so on which meant so much to them would likely fall victim to the systematic theft among baggage handlers, who would now have greater opportunities to steal consumer electronics.

These supposed connections between the humble MP3 player and international terrorism underline the connectivity of the globalised world and all its technologies, including those which are associated with the apparently harmless practices involved in making and listening to music. This book explores the current state and potential futures of music, its producers and consumers, and the industries which support it in this globalised, multimedia, and very anxious world. This means dealing with the changing flows of sound, including the availability of so much music to so many people – which in turn means looking at changes in music's relationship with business structures, money, technology, and consumer choice in a world changing with bewildering rapidity. It also means assessing the impact of these changes on the ways in which we think about 'music'.

Let us start to explore this question. 'Music' is a phenomenon which can be considered and enjoyed in and for itself. But in the capitalist world it has been made until recently in conditions of mass production. The resulting products – CDs, DVDs, and so on – are bought, sold and 'consumed' much like any other mass commodity, to the regret of many composers, performers and listeners who like to think of music as a very special category of human endeavour, which is or should be beyond the merely economic in value. However, the existing relationship between music and the flow of capital was in fact threatened in the last quarter of the twentieth century by the increasing difficulties of the partnership between the producers of recordings for sale, and the makers of the equipment which reproduces those recordings.

This partnership, necessary as it was, had never worked entirely smoothly. Throughout the twentieth century discrete objects such as vinyl singles or CD albums were produced by a manufacturer (a record label) who held copyright on behalf of composer and performer, and expected to be paid each time a copy of the recording was either bought or broadcast. The recording and broadcasting industries, meanwhile, had developed carriers of musical information (from recording tape to hard-disk-sharing internet software) through which music could be copied, erased and re-used without further payment to the makers of the original product. In other words one part of the music industry provided commodities which allowed the domestic user to copy commercial recordings without respecting the copyrights held by the other part of the music industry. As these technologies developed to allow more perfect copying and wider sharing, they threatened to destabilise what the record companies saw as the 'value' of music.

There were other challenges to the agreed 'value' of music. During the twentieth century jazz, rock, soul and many other 'popular' music genres were taken increasingly seriously by critics and public alike. So, certainly from the 1960s onwards, it became difficult to defend a hierarchy of musical value in which the best music was assumed to be the life's work of a small number of European composers, most of whom were long dead. As Ian MacDonald argued in *Revolution in the Head*, an influential book about the Beatles, there was indeed a 'revolution in the head' which encouraged people to challenge this deference to the cultural materials of the past, and rock music, partly led by the obvious qualities of the Liverpool quartet's achievements, was in the vanguard of the challenge.

In another sense, though, Anglo-American rock music was very old-fashioned. Performers played to paying audiences whose participation was limited to singing along; almost all of their music – songs, mainly – followed the harmonic and melodic rules of existing Western and African-American music; and they wrote and recorded within strict format limits, such as the time available on a vinyl single. Rock music journalists, acting in the same way as classical music or theatre critics employed by the more upmarket newspapers, arranged their work in a hierarchy of value which echoed those lists of old European composers. The lists changed every so often – for example, in the mid-1970s punk replaced progressive rock in importance for some listeners, and most critics – but it was a hierarchy of value none the less.

Several things upset the new order. Firstly, African-American and African-Caribbean music diversified away from their blues and gospel roots; dub reggae and hip-hop began to order sounds in ways which were very different from the compositional and improvisational styles of jazz, soul, pop or rock. Secondly, music from elsewhere in the world became increasingly available, and increasingly influential in the West. Thirdly, the dance musics of the mid-1980s undermined both the traditional performer–audience relationship and the traditional ways of listening to music. This was music to dream to, to drift in and out of contact with – but not to listen to (or perform) with the same kind of concentration as folk, jazz, soul or rock. It became easier to think of music as a form of narcotic, perhaps less easy to think of it as the centrepiece of people's identities. The invasive, and cumulative, cultural impact of dance music can be heard in the BBC news theme which was composed by David Lowe for an October 1999 programme rebrand (and has been rearranged by him many times thereafter for other BBC news programming such as the BBC News 24 channel). It is a short piece of repetitive, trancey, dance music which cleverly uses percussion instruments to prefigure the 'pips' which signal the hour on BBC radio and television news services.

It is entirely possible that this kind of floating interaction with music *is* a defensive response to its pervasiveness. We might be able to concentrate for an hour or so on actively listening, but since music is so pervasive, so completely and universally available, we can no longer choose when to do so. But many of us still want music to have meaning. In his interesting 1998 book *Techgnosis*, Erik Davis reminded us that the spiritual and the technological have always been, and still are, intertwined, and he insists that if we are to continue to glean *meaning* from the overwhelming amount of musical *information*, they'd better remain so. We have to learn not just to surf, says Davis, but to thresh and glean, in order to make meaning from the vast amounts of information available. To underline the point Davis makes one of a number of striking musical analogies. 'We must learn to think like DJs, sampling texts and voices from a vast cornucopia of records while staying true to the organic demands of the dance' (Davis 1998 p.332). In the digital age, everyone involved in the making and use of music must learn to think (and act) in this way.

Many people already do just this, by making and using music on their computers. Leaving aside the controversial issue of illegal file sharing, some people would see fans' remix cultures as harbingers of a genuinely new musical democracy. This may be so – and such arguments are explored at length below – but they are at least as much a replacement for traditional instrumental performance, and for the traditional band, which was and remains a form of semi-independent (if usually masculine) socialisation. Commonly available music programmes such as Apple's GarageBand and Sony's ACID xPress offer the user a number of pre-recorded loops to choose from, and simply re-ordering them constitutes a new piece of music. Such programmes inviting the re-creation and re-use of existing digitally encoded music indicate that we have

x

to think hard about what concepts like 'originality' and 'creativity' might mean in this context. 'We must all learn to think and act like DJs', and anyone who uses a composition package such as *GarageBand* or *ACID xPress* is already doing so.

In another sense, though – as the name *GarageBand* implies – this practice is only a new *articulation* of a traditional practice of music education and composition, which has always taken existing music as its starting point. The isolated teenager making new musical collages as an entry into creativity, and spreading them through file sharing, personalised Web2 pages on the internet, and/or mobile phone jamming, is acting in a similar way as his/her predecessors, who would listen to, copy from and transform music from vinyl records and radio broadcasts, share these interests at school or college, and possibly form a band and rehearse in a garage. Even through the relatively private worlds of portable MP3 players, solo-composition packages such as *GarageBand*, and the internet, music still offers strong cultural cement. But, in order for music to continue to operate in this way, certain kinds of music-making – including the new – will need sustained encouragement.

Chapter one

From wax to DACs: the rise and rise of popular music

This first chapter reflects on how we got here. It looks at the growth of commercial popular musics based on broadcasting and recording; at the rise to global dominance of Anglo-American rock, pop, and black musics since the 1950s, and the subsequent rise of music from elsewhere in the world since the 1980s; and at the changing place of music in audio-visual entertainment. All this, together with the technological developments of the digital era, has produced an era of musical abundance: so much recorded music is now available that no-one could possibly listen to it all, and in fact many of us have more music on our iPods than we could ever listen to. So, how *did* we get to here?

Music made or inspired by black Americans impacted on the world in the early twentieth century, and especially in the 1920s. This was the decade after the long and terribly destructive First World War had weakened public confidence in European economies and culture alike. Thanks to the new technologies of recording and broadcasting, the new musical genres of jazz, ragtime and blues became popular in much of Europe in the early twentieth century, and they brought with them a host of pleasurable and slightly dangerous associations. Popular music, sex, the narcotic pleasures of illegal drugs, and the bohemian lifestyles of childless young adults were irretrievably mixed in the popular imagination even in the 1920s. Contemporary 'celebrity culture', fuelled by tabloid newspaper reporting of the sex, drugs and rock'n'roll lifestyles of the rich and famous, continues this association.

Nonetheless there was, and is, more to popular music than the glamorous life of the urban young. Even in the 1920s, jazz was a *commercial* music, tied to those mass communication technologies of broadcasting and recording; and during the twentieth century these new broadcast media also made available popular songs and dances from a variety of other American and European traditions such as Broadway vaudeville and Hollywood musicals, the French chanson, Austro-German light opera, and the British music-hall song. Each of these was less subversive than the new musics of the 1920s, appealing across generation and gender to the mass consumerism of 'family entertainment', and although there was a series of faddish dance musics (such as the big band 'swing' popularised worldwide by the Glenn Miller band in the early 1940s, or the 'twist' in the early 1960s) which were taken up enthusiastically by the young, most commercial popular music fell squarely into the bracket of general family entertainment.

Outside and beyond the realms of commercial music, local rural traditions of music-making remained important even in industrialised nations, and the industrial working classes had also made and shared songs about their lives which were a world away from the 'Moon in June' lyrics of the average commercial popular song. However, all these 'folk' music and dancing traditions were seen to be in decline, threatened by the national cultures of broadcasting and the globalising tendencies of the gramophone. As a result, all over the world, from the start of the twentieth century, folk songs and dances were collected by earnest enthusiasts, and archives of transcriptions and recordings were built up. In the Communist countries which were formed in the Russian sphere of influence after the Second World War, traditional songs and dances were used as a means of promoting and conserving an official national identity. Similarly, in the UK and the USA in the 1950s the traditions of folk performance were revived by Communists such as Ewan McColl and Pete Seeger who believed that these songs represented the authentic voice of the people. By contrast, they believed that commercial popular music was harmful to their political cause, because individualised love songs distracted working people from reflecting on the real problems of their conditions of existence.

Meanwhile, despite these attempts to preserve, promote and politicise local and national cultures, the commercial American music industry continued to prosper. In those post-war years musicals, jazz and big-band swing were in decline, but rock'n'roll made a big impact around most of the world, and the new music divided the public for commercial popular music along generational lines once more. At this point, therefore – the mid-1950s – commentators noted the advent of the 'teenager', who was a cause of concern to the authorities (since teenagers tended to hang around together, they were thought to experiment with sex and illegal narcotic drugs, and they were sometimes involved in social violence, often following rock'n'roll concerts). At the same time the teenager was recognised as a new category of consumer (teenagers often had money to spend, and only themselves to spend it on).

The music business provided a new, relatively cheap, format – the seven-inch vinyl 'single' – and new music – rock'n'roll, and then in the early 1960s 'pop' – for these new big spenders. The fashion industry also provided mass-market but distinctively styled clothing for teenagers and young adults with disposable income, and partly as a result the first 'subcultures' emerged – groups of young people with aggressively shared tastes in new styles of music and clothing, usually a shared preference for a particular drug, and always a shared distaste for their parents' values and for authority more generally. Members of subcultures like the 'mods' of early-1960s Britain were closely tied to their generation. After a few years, another group of youngsters would emerge, wearing different clothing, listening to a different genre of music, and often indulging in a different narcotic or psychedelic drug of choice, much to the

2

consternation of the popular newspapers. Because of this cyclical media concern (sometimes called a 'moral panic'), people who wrote about youth subcultures have often claimed that they were somehow 'resisting' the values of the dominant culture.

There was more to subcultures than generational tension or lurid newspaper stories about youth misbehaviour. One of the first writers to discuss the phenomenon within the UK, Dick Hebdige, described subcultures as a 'phantom dialogue' between black and white cultures, a dialogue focused around dress and music, and embracing the marginality of non-white cultures against mainstream whiteness. There seems to be a good deal of truth in this description if we look at the evolution of popular music. Like jazz and swing before it, both rock'n'roll and a great deal of the Anglo-American pop of the late 1950s and early 1960s were made either by black American artists such as Chuck Berry, Bo Diddley, Little Richard, Diana Ross or Aretha Franklin, or by white American artists such as singers Elvis Presley and Buddy Holly who were clearly influenced by African-American music, or by white British bands like the Animals and the Rolling Stones, who openly acknowledged the influence of African-American blues and rhythm'n'blues.

Some of the music made by white artists was less obviously African-American in influence. The early 1960s pop singles charts were full of records by singers like Connie Francis, Frankie Vaughan and Neil Sedaka, whose songwriters worked in the tradition of popular song established in the 1930s, and other traditions were, and remain, in evidence. In Britain the popular songs of 'music hall' were part of the background of bands such as the Beatles, Madness, and Squeeze, and you can even trace this music hall legacy in the witty half-spoken lyrics of early twenty-first century acts such as The Streets and the Arctic Monkeys. British folksong traditions were important to bands like Steeleye Span, Pentangle and in their later years Led Zeppelin; even the Rolling Stones track 'Lady Jane' (1966) is more of a folk ballad than a rock'n'roll song. Classical music was also influential: for a few years (roughly 1969–74) 'progressive rock' bands like Yes and Emerson Lake and Palmer (and a bunch of less well-known bands such as Caravan, Soft Machine and Hatfield and the North) flirted with some of the techniques of classical music, playing long compositions with difficult rhythms and obscure lyrics. But even with these progressive rock bands the sounds, rhythms and harmonies of blues, jazz and soul were never too far away, and they continued to provide the basic structural and sonic material for almost all pop, rock and heavy metal. If you listened to the Beatles or Led Zeppelin, in other words, you would probably hear the African-American tradition as a more obvious influence than music hall or folk music.

The 'phantom dialogue' has continued: in the mid-1970s punk musicians played alongside reggae bands; the British and European electronic pop and

3

dance music of the later 1980s (most of it made by white men) owed a great deal to the soundworlds and technological innovations made largely by black American men: the first generation of New York based hip-hop artists, and the electronic dance musics made in Chicago (House) and Detroit (Techno).

Something else has happened since that moment of musical and cultural innovation in the late 1980s. The people who followed those new electronic dance musics (House, Techno, and the many forms which have been derived from them) seemed to form a new subculture. They dressed alike; they participated in new forms of social organisation such as free parties in warehouses or large open-air spaces; and they took the newly fashionable psychotropic drug MDMA or Ecstasy. In a way they were also political, since many of them demonstrated in defence of 'the right to party' in the early 1990s, when UK legislation threatened to take away that right. Since this point, however, there has been far less generational innovation and far more of the recycling of musical styles and forms of dress. So musical genres such as the 'Britpop' of the mid-1990s, or 'nu-metal' and the new 'r'n'b' in the later 1990s, owed a great deal to previous styles, and for all that they were marketed to (and appealed to) young people, they did not produce new subcultures as such. Indeed, many of the most enthusiastic followers of Britpop bands like Blur, Oasis and Pulp were older people who liked the familiar guitar-based sounds, and songs with deliberate echoes of the pop of the mid-1960s. This recycling of mass culture across the generations seemed to signal the end of youth culture or subculture as a progressive generational revelation, in the West at any rate. Meanwhile in the late 1990s, following the global success of the Spice Girls, chart pop was aimed not at teenagers but at pre-teen girls or 'tweenagers', and in the early years of the new century, manufactured pop became part of reality television (through shows such as *Pop Idol* and *American Idol*), and it seemed that for the time being chart pop had safely been returned to family entertainment.

Popular music in the global village

It may not be surprising then that, as innovation in Anglo-American music began to run out of steam, many people living in the West turned their attention to music made elsewhere. In some cases this meant making music which was connected with wherever they or their parents had lived before coming to the West. In the UK, for instance, music culture was significantly changed because of the immigration of large numbers of Commonwealth people into British cities which began in the 1950s; people came from parts of Africa, South Asia, and the West Indian islands. Thanks to the new mix of people and cultures, British cities produced waves of new music in club/dance culture and guitar rock alike. Ska made a modest impact on the pop charts of the early 1960s, and in the 1970s British-based labels like Island and Trojan made reggae into a global music. Meanwhile dub, which was pioneered in

Jamaica by King Tubby and developed in Britain by people such as the producer Adrian Sherwood, working with bands like African Headcharge, was crucial to the mid-1990s development of the post-techno electronic dance form drum'n'bass. In reggae, rock and pop there is a long line of 'mixed race' bands in the UK, from the Coventry-based 'two-tone' bands like The Special AKA and The Selecter, or Birmingham reggae band UB40 in the 1970s, through London pop groups such as Culture Club and the Thompson Twins in early 1980s pop, to Bristol's Massive Attack, whose jazz-funk, soul and dub samples and contemporary lyrical references explored the urban melting pot of the 1990s, as did the aggressive stadium rock of Skunk Anansie.

5

Having been successfully reverse-colonised by people from the Caribbean, musical Britain also became partly Asian in the 1990s. The guitarist Nitin Sawhney moved serenely between North Indian forms and jazz, and composed soundtrack scores for film and television; the 'indie' (independent-label) pop of Cornershop, led by Tjinder Singh, and the eccentric musings of White Town (Jyoti Mishra, who recorded his 1997 hit single 'Your Woman' using a home computer and an audio cassette multi-track tape recorder) made it into the mainstream pop charts. Singer Sheila Chandra created a hybrid spirituality on a number of albums for the Real World label (and a reputation so wide that she made a contribution to the soundtrack of Peter Jackson's 2002 blockbuster movie *The Lord of the Rings: The Two Towers*); Bally Sagoo explored the byways of Bollywood film music, heard through ears used to the new dance music, and in 1996 his 'Dil Cheez' was the first song in Hindi to appear in the British pop charts. Talvin Singh also made music for the dance world, and won the prestigious Mercury Music Prize in 1999 for his album *OK*. More controversially in some people's ears, in an echo of the take-up of Indian instrumental sounds in the 1960s by the Beatles, Quintessence and others, white middle-class band Kula Shaker produced a hippyish, Hindu-influenced Britpop, complete with sitar and tabla providing atmosphere behind the guitars.

All this is a huge qualifier to Dick Hebdige's idea of the 'phantom dialogue' as a driver for the cyclical emergence of youth subcultures – actually, there was and is a very un-ghostly, face-to-face dialogue in the UK, and it had been going for quite a while before Hebdige's model was first proposed in 1978. The model assumes that a majority of white and a minority of black people live in virtually separate worlds. In the USA they often were, with racist record companies calling blues, jazz and soul 'race music' and racist radio stations which only broadcast the work of white or black artists. This pattern of discrimination even applied to MTV in its first few years in the early 1980s, which had an unspoken white-only policy before the global success of Michael Jackson's 1984 album *Thriller* forced the station to play black music videos (and there's a similar story with hip-hop, which took too long to become regularly featured on the channel). But the UK is not quite the same as the USA, for two principal reasons.

Firstly, most of the black people who arrived in the UK in the 1950s–1990s came there not from the USA but from the islands of the Caribbean; they were already involved in a dialogue of their own with black American culture. The relaxed lilt of Trinidadian calypso and soca, and the stricter rhythms of Jamaican 'rocksteady' and 'ska' of the early 1960s, like the more laid-back rhythms of reggae which developed from ska during the following decade, indicate that black people from the Caribbean did not simply mimic American music, but developed their own in response to it – this dialogue is an aspect of the cultural exchange which Paul Gilroy has called the Black Atlantic.

Secondly, just as with jazz from the 1920s onwards (and rather more than in American popular music), in UK popular music white people and people of colour have often worked alongside each other and together, within a culture which is less obviously racist than that of the USA. The Jimi Hendrix Experience, for example, was formed by a black American living in London and two white Brits, and it made music which still has massive resonance today. Hendrix was living in London partly in order to make music in a less racist environment: he wasn't expected to play rhythm'n'blues or any other black genre, and it was therefore easier for him to become a rock star, alongside contemporary white British virtuoso guitarists (and blues worshippers) such as Eric Clapton or Jeff Beck. The result of this less divided society, then, is a popular music which has less firm 'racial' divisions than the version over the pond. Having said that, the UK music business is not and never has been an anti-racist utopia; for example, it is probably true that the UK record industry has consistently under-invested in black artists as compared with white artists.

Meanwhile as well as various changes in the *production* of music towards the expression of a changing, broadening musical culture, there was also a significant change in the Western *consumption* of music: to put it simply, people started listening to and buying more music from outside the Anglo-American pop/rock/soul mainstream. Popular music outside the West had always been made, bought and sold, of course, but by the 1980s it was more widely available in the USA and Western Europe. One response was a new way of categorising all popular music which was not directly Anglo-American in inspiration (though many of its practitioners live(d) in the West). The term 'world music' was invented in the late 1980s at a meeting in London of people who ran record labels specialising in such non-Western popular music. 'World music' was therefore not an analytical category, or even a description of a certain type of sound, but a commodity category – in other words, it was used to make it easier for shops to catalogue, stock and sell these products. It was not an adequate description of musics as different as the Zimbabwean guitar pop of the Bhundu Boys and the Bulgarian choir music of the bestselling 1988 album *Mystères des Voix Bulgares*, each of which sold very well in the late 1980s as the new term 'world music' was coming into use.

Since then perhaps because of the descriptive inadequacy of 'world music', it has been joined by another word, 'roots', which is less a commodity category and more a way of describing the ways in which local 'folk' musics have developed under the pressures of global cultural contact, while trying to remain connected to their own traditions. The Finnish band Värttinä, for example, started in the early 1980s intent on preserving a particular type of popular song for women's voices, with an accompanying ensemble of acoustic instruments, which comes from the Western Finnish province of Karelia. The members of the band firstly played and sang existing songs in this tradition, then started to compose their own songs, which at first added to this repertoire in the same style (for example much of the 1991 album *Oi Dai*) and then moved slowly away from it to acknowledge the influence of other traditional and popular musics (starting with the album *Seleniko*, which was produced in 1992 by Hijaz Mustapha, the founder of the pioneering world music band Three Mustaphas Three and owner of the London-based label Globestyle Records). Increasingly since that point, Värttinä have used amplified rock instruments in the accompanying ensemble, and they have also engaged with electronic dance music (e.g. on the 1997 album *Kokko*). They have collaborated with Bollywood composer A.R. Rahman in the development of the music for the staged version of J.R.R. Tolkien's epic story *The Lord of the Rings*. So, while it started as a 'folk' band, Värttinä has become not a folk but a 'roots' band, composing and performing music which is rooted in folk traditions but not tied to them. Meanwhile, despite singing in Finnish, the band has developed a global fan base, most of whom can happily sing along to the lyrics at Värttinä's gigs, even if they don't understand a word of them.

This way of using tradition, changing but not abandoning it, was particularly important to the nations of Eastern Europe as they emerged from the Communist era during the 1990s. In most of these countries national folk traditions were identified with the oppressive regimes of the post-war era before 1989, while Anglo-American pop, rock and jazz were seen as musics of resistance to the dominant culture and were often banned or otherwise driven underground – punk rock had performed this function in Poland, as did the music of acts like Velvet Underground and Frank Zappa in the former Czechoslovakia. Since the end of the Russian Empire in 1989, a number of bands have developed a 'global music' to fit the new Eastern Europe in which global trade and migration are increasingly important, and in which the dominant musical forces have become freely available. Polish band Brathanki, for example, have evolved a very inclusive musicality which references a wide range of genres from Polish and Hungarian folk and composed musics, through pop, reggae, jazz and rock. Listen, for instance, to the treatments of their recurring, brief, 'Brathanki' theme tune in the 2000 album *Ano!*, which includes versions in folk-choral, New Orleans jazz, disco and country styles. In the autumn of 2000 this album was one place above Britney Spears' *Oops!...I*

7

did it Again on the Polish album charts. Brathanki were at that point signed to the local Columbia label – which is owned by Sony, whose company philosophy is indeed encapsulated by the key phrase 'global localisation', now often abbreviated to 'glocalisation'. The Britney Spears album is on Jive Records, also part of the Sony record label group.

Another form many of whose musicians are very aware of its own history is jazz. This music has stopped evolving principally as an American form; indeed, some people would now say that it is no longer innovative in its USA birthplace (where it is often taught alongside classical music as a set of established performance techniques; here perhaps the history of the music does trap younger performers into reproducing rather than innovating). Meanwhile, it seems, jazz is continuing to evolve precisely as a 'foreign language'. Jazz has been honoured as an art form in Europe since the 1920s, indeed it was, arguably, always taken more seriously in Europe than in the USA, and consequently American musicians such as clarinet and sax player Sidney Bechet and saxophonist Dexter Gordon spent much of their working lives in Europe. Many Europeans learned to play jazz with a high level of proficiency. However, apart from the work of the guitarist Django Reinhardt (1910–53) and his band the Quintet of the Hot Club of France, on the whole European jazz before the 1960s was a polite, enthusiastic and careful imitation of whatever the Americans were doing rather than a genuinely innovative contribution to the evolution of the music. Europeans played swing, be-bop, hard bop, and in the early 1960s they enthusiastically built a 'trad jazz' revival of the 1920s New Orleans style, which even got British artists like clarinettist Acker Bilk and trumpeter Kenny Ball some chart success in the USA; but on the whole the Europeans did not play a jazz of their own.

In the 1960s there was more genuine innovation among European jazz musicians, though in one direction this was more important to the musicians involved than to any potential audience. Taking as their starting point the relatively aggressive, improvisatory 'free jazz' pioneered in the USA by players such as Ornette Coleman and John Coltrane, European improvisers went further and faster, working out new ways of playing, and listening to each other, which broke most of the accepted rules of performance. Leading lights of this new music included the guitarist Derek Bailey, the saxophonists Evan Parker and Peter Brotzmann, and the percussionist Han Bennink.

Free improvisation was not the only innovation; it was matched by pioneering multicultural crossovers such as the Indo-Jazz Fusions, a band led, in London, by the Jamaican saxophonist Joe Harriott and the Indian violinist John Mayer. The musical direction of this band's two late-1960s albums were echoed a few years later in the very multinational projects led by guitarist John McLaughlin, such as the virtuoso jazz-rock of the Mahavishnu Orchestra (which toured and recorded during 1970–6) and the more contemplative, mainly acoustic sounds of the band Shakti (which toured and recorded during 1975–7, and subsequently reformed as Remember Shakti), in which Indian musicians playing traditional instruments appeared alongside McLaughlin's acoustic guitar (a practice subsequently echoed in the USA by guitarist Lee Boice, whose recordings have featured Ustad Sultan Khan playing sarangi and Gadal Roy, who has often worked with McLaughlin, playing tabla). Both of the 1970s McLaughlin-led projects anticipated by over a decade the 'fusion' element of 'world music', which has seen the development of a number of deliberately cross-cultural musical experiments such as Afro Celt Sound System, which was founded in 1992 with British, African and Irish membership, and has made a number of albums mixing African and Celtic rhythms and melodies with elements of dance electronica and jazz.

In his provocatively titled 2006 book *Is Jazz Dead?* Stuart Nicholson has argued that the most interesting and original jazz is now made outside the USA, in Africa, in Latin America and – especially – in Northern Europe, where a host of relatively small, independent labels such as ECM promote the music of Scandinavian composer/performers such as guitarist Terje Rypdal, saxophonist Jan Garbarek, and bands like the pianist Tord Gustavsen's Trio, or Nordic, another piano-bass-drums trio led by pianist Bugge Wesseltoft. These musicians engage with all their local traditions of music-making (including folk performance and classical composition) as well as with the history of American jazz, its performing styles and its 'standards'.

In some parts of the world locally made popular music from mainstream genres tends to be sung in English. Much (but not all) Swedish and Finnish pop, whether dance music, indie-style songs or heavy metal, is sung in English. Although most of the market for Scandinavian pop in English is in fact in its countries of origin, performing songs in English has helped Swedish dance-pop bands like ABBA, Roxette and Ace of Base, and the Finnish gothic-metal-lite bands HIM (His Infernal Majesty) and Nightwish to become international successes; Lordi, another Finnish metal-lite band, even won the normally ultra-bland Eurovision Song Contest in 2006. Nonetheless there is also a great deal of 'local' pop, rock, metal and hip-hop which is sung in languages other than English – including some music made in the USA or in Latin America with words in Spanish, and music made in England and India with words in Punjabi or Hindi, but also some Swedish pop and Finnish heavy metal – which has little or nothing to do with the local or ethnic traditions implied in 'world' or 'roots', but is in both soundworld and lyrical content Anglo-American music sung in another language.

However, whatever the language of delivery and the source of the genre, most music has some local flavour. France, for example, is often claimed to be the second-largest market after the USA for hip-hop music; and most of the hip-hop sold in France is French. The most popular French-language rapper, Dakar-born Parisian MC Solaar, has averaged sales of over a million copies per album, while in 1994 the single 'Je Danse la Mia' by IAM reached number one in the French charts. Rap acts have been regular winners of major awards for achievement in popular music in France since the mid-1990s. The annual *Victoires de la Musique* award for best male artist went to MC Solaar in 1995, while in 1998 IAM's *L'École du micro d'argent* was named album of the year. However, since 2000 the category of overall 'album of the year' has been abandoned, and rappers are now judged in a category which lumps together most current genres within black popular music, including rap alongside ragga, hip-hop and r'n'b.

As Rupa Huq has shown, rap is popular in France well beyond the troubled suburbs of Paris and Marseilles with their ethnic minority communities, partly because it is *not* simply a copy of the American model. Francophone rap is seen as part of the defence of the French language in the face of the creeping and much-feared Anglicisation which can be seen in such common French phrases as 'le weekend'. (This defence has also been manifested in the legal provision of a 40 per cent quota of Francophone output for radio stations, and a similar attitude to Anglo-Americanisation is apparent in the legal challenge to the iPod's copy-protection software, and the relationship between the iPod and the iTunes music sales, recording and transfer system, which was enacted into French law in early 2006.)

Rap is also important elsewhere in Europe (and in the rest of the world – the Transrap website boasts significant hip-hop cultures in 167 countries in all). It's a particularly flourishing form in Italy, Germany – especially among Germans of Turkish origin – and Switzerland. Most writers on European rap agree that rap has become de-Americanised and taken on aspects of the local – it's a good example of the way in which 'global' forms can exist as expressive of local cultures. Rap in Italy, for example, is widely agreed to be more genuinely, that is culturally, 'Italian' than Italian rock music, most of which sounds very American even when the words are in Italian. Tony Mitchell's study of rap in southern Italy brings this out clearly. Mitchell examines the music's local histories and rivalries, its relation to traditional forms such as Neapolitan folksong, the local improvised poetry form *ottava rima*, and even seventeenth century opera recitative (where the singers half-speak, half-sing over a very fluid musical accompaniment), in just the same way that French rappers locate their raps as aspects of the French traditions of poetry and chanson.

As well as using languages such as Hindi and Punjabi, most popular music in India has had some sort of sonic base in local music; even with the out-and-out pop of India's first manufactured boy band, the cunningly titled Band of Boys, dhol and tabla drums, playing traditional rhythmic patterns against the more synthetic global pop sounds, provide obvious continuity with the musics of the past. Similarly, in Pakistan, popular music has included the ghazal (Qawwali) crossover of the singer Nusret Fateh Ali Khan, but also the mildly controversial, political 'sufi-pop' of Junoon; as with Brathanki and Värttinä, these artists' music owes as much to tradition as to modernity. However, as the forces of globalisation take hold in India (whose economy has grown almost as rapidly as China's since protectionism was ended in the 1990s), the various blends of Indian beats and western pop harmonies known loosely as 'Indi-Pop', and the equally hybrid musics of Bollywood film soundtracks and new-age crossovers from Indian classical music, have been joined by a more aggressively Western-sounding Indian rock, made by bands such as Thermal and a Quarter, Zero, and Indus Creed (who recorded their first album in Los Angeles).

11

These examples, including the use of an LA recording studio, should emphasise the impossibility of cultural separateness within the global musical world. Music from almost anywhere is available almost everywhere else – and so are people. There are now significant populations of South Asian origin – by 'South Asia' is meant India, Pakistan, Bangladesh and Sri Lanka – in the USA, Canada, and the UK; indeed, there are so many people of South Asian origin in the USA that there is a specific MTV channel for them. Similarly, India-based music journalism recognises and celebrates the horizontal geography of 'Indian' music, discussing the music made by South Asians in London and New York as eagerly as it reviews music made in Delhi by Indian citizens and touring UK-born musicians alike. For example, there was heated controversy in the online magazine *Indian Music* over *Come Away with Me* (2002), the first album by Norah Jones, the New York-born and Texas-bred daughter of the popular sitar virtuoso Ravi Shankar. The controversy was not only about whether or in what sense Norah Jones might be considered 'Indian', but equally about whether or in what sense (if any) the album, which was released on the jazz-specialist Blue Note label, could be called 'jazz'.

South Asians in many other parts of the world have developed their own musical variants on inherited tradition through interaction with other available musical materials and performing techniques. In the West Indian island Trinidad, for example, which has a significant population of South Asian origin, a relentlessly upbeat genre called 'Chutney' exists as an Indianised version of the local dance music, Soca (which is itself a blend of American 'soul' – what we would now call r'n'b – and the indigenous 'calypso'). In the UK, perhaps the longest-lasting of these innovations has been Bhangra, which is based on a Punjabi folk music style, but uses electric guitars and keyboards alongside the dhol drums. Partly because of its continuing use of lyrics in the Punjabi language, in the 1980s Bhangra developed a whole economy of its own, with videos, records and CDs which were made and distributed by small businesses rather than major record labels, and sold in local Asian food or clothing shops rather than mainstream record stores (and therefore sales did not register in the pop charts). There is also a Bhangra concert and party circuit which is often focused on 'all-dayers' aimed at young people whose parents would not let them stay out at night. A similar phenomenon known as Joi Bangla emerged, also in and after the 1980s, among young East London residents of Bangladeshi origin; the musical lead was taken by brothers Farook and Haroon Shamsher, a.k.a. Joi, whose credits include music for the computer game *The Chaos Engine* (the first version was released in 1993) as well as dance music.

As noted above, during the 1990s South Asian music and musicians became a routine part of the British music industry: indeed, people such as Apache Indian, Bally Sagoo, Najma Akhtar, and Jay Sean have each made a contribution and been dropped by or left major record labels, while younger musicians have emerged for their own short careers in the limelight. This dropping has been claimed to be part of a racist industry which exploited Indians as an exotic fashion and then got rid of them once public taste had shifted. While this might be substantially true, it could equally be argued that this kind of shoddy treatment of artists by record companies is perfectly normal: most musicians in popular music, whatever their ethnicity, have short and not very lucrative careers.

The great exception to this rule – the South Asian with the great rock career, an archetype imagined wistfully in Salman Rushdie's underrated 1999 novel *The Ground Beneath Her Feet* – has in fact already happened. Freddie Mercury, the iconic lead singer of stadium rock band Queen, whose 1975 hit 'Bohemian Rhapsody' helped to invent the rock video, was born in 1947 to Indian parents of the Zoroastrian faith (which is Persian in origin). For whatever reason, at the height of his fame Mercury – whose original name was Farok Bulsara – chose to be identified as Persian rather than Indian. The family moved to England in 1963, where Mercury completed his education, changed his name, and formed Queen with college friends Roger Taylor and Brian May. Queen represents the new geography of popular music just as effectively as Cornershop.

Queen, on the other hand, were a rock band with very few musical resonances outside the Anglo-American mainstream (in their case including classical music and especially opera). Generic survival, revival, and innovation remain more likely in the smaller labels than with the few global players, and among small-label sites on the internet as well as in shops; indeed, according to American punk rock label Epitaph Records the very survival of the music they record and sell is due to the global market which the World Wide Web has created. So, in a form which was largely discarded by the major labels and mass media in around 1980, punk rock by the likes of the Dead Kennedys and the Dropkick Murphys has survived in a market which is fragmented and discontinuous but also global, as it is with recordings of locally and ethnically specific musics which originate from outside the West.

These local musics sell to known audiences, including major 'multicultural' Western cities, but as often they serve local populations through intermediate technology. Cheap to buy and to copy to and from, the compact audio cassette was developed by Philips in the 1960s first for use in dictation machines, then as a modest alternative to the reel-to-reel recording tape developed in the 1940s, which was used by the recording industry and favoured by the hi-fi enthusiast. Indeed, the smaller format's indifferent sonic capability meant that few specialist hi-fi manufacturers attempted to make high-quality cassette playback/recording machines (one Japanese firm, Nakamichi, filled that gap in the market to the virtual exclusion of others). But the cassette's cheapness as a medium – with equally cheap playback machines readily available – simultaneously helped the exposure of the rest of the world to Anglo-American pop, and enabled small recording and manufacturing operations, recording local music, to challenge the majors' hegemony.

The compact cassette did not, however, necessarily benefit local markets. By the end of the 1970s both EMI and Decca had withdrawn from Ghana thanks to local cassette cultures, which were copying commercial tapes illegally for retail; consequently, by the end of the 1980s, there was no Ghanaian recording industry beyond the craft stage. In India, on the other hand, low-cost cassette-based recording labels were unambiguously a success story. They flourished in the last quarter of the century, where India's biggest label, the local (i.e. Indian-owned) HMV, saw its proportion of all recorded music sales (mainly of Bollywood film scores with songs in Hindi) fall from 80 per cent to less than 15 per cent during the 1980s; while PolyGram's Music India label sold about eight per cent, most of the rest were by small-scale, low-cost labels, serving the tastes of local or regional genres and languages. The gradual growth of CDs in India in the 1990s posed little threat of a comeback either by major labels or Bollywood, as by the later 1990s CD players, writers and media were almost as low in price as cassettes and their recorder/players.

The survival of local music industries has as often been due to governmental strategy as to the operations of market forces. In most of the Communist world, classical and folk musics were propagated officially, through broadcasts on state radio, and recordings by state-sanctioned ensembles sold through labels such as Hungaroton (Hungary), Electrecord (Romania) and Melodiya (Russia). Two examples from Communist-era Romania's Electrecord label, each released in 1977, indicate the range of official musical discourses which were supported by the regime. One album contains George Enescu's Rapsodia Română nos. 1 and 2, op. 11, alongside his *Poema* Română, op. 1, played by the Symphony Orchestra of Romanian Radio conducted by Iosif Conta; the album's sleevenotes earnestly document Enescu's place at the head of the 'Romanian School' of classical composition (the record number is ST-ECE 0817). Another record presents Dumitru Farcaș, with a small instrumental ensemble, playing Transylvanian folk music on the clarinet-like instrument the taragot; here, the sleeve quotes at length from approving reviews of Farcas's playing in German, Swiss and French newspapers (ST-EPE 01334). Electrecord did not, however, release any Romanian jazz, pop or rock.

In this context jazz and rock music, which were often dismissed as bourgeois decadence by official Communist propaganda, often had a genuinely subversive existence. Vaclav Havel, the leader of the Czechoslovakian 'Velvet Revolution' of 1989, and subsequently the first president of the new Czech Republic, stressed the importance of the Czech rock underground led by acts such as Plastic People, and their Western models such as the Velvet Underground, to the eventual defeat of Communism. After coming to power Havel asked that the libertarian composer, bandleader and rock guitar hero Frank Zappa be allowed to act as American cultural attaché to Eastern Europe (the American political elite recoiled in horror and the request was refused), while the Rolling Stones were so impressed by the beauty of the city they saw when they played their first gig in the Czech capital, Prague, that they helped to fund the post-Communist restoration of the city centre.

While Anglo-American music only became a fully available commodity in Eastern Europe after 1989, in much of the Western world locally made music was almost as fiercely protected as it was in Eastern Europe, though in this case it was protected as a commodity as well as cultural archaeology. Public policy in Britain from the 1930s to the 1960s fostered local popular-musical cultures which were Americanised in style but British in personnel. The Musicians' Union, the trade union of the profession, exercised control over the number of performances by visiting Americans; visitors were only allowed to perform in the UK if the same number of British artists performed in the USA. The union also negotiated a series of 'needle time' agreements with the BBC, which controlled the amount of time that broadcasters could give to recordings, thus maintaining the employment of local musicians. The legendary 'John Peel Sessions' which ran on the Radio One DJ's programme from 1967 till his untimely death in 2004 are among the more positive results of this form of cultural control – as, arguably, was the growth of a distinctively British pop; it is hard to imagine the emergence of the Beatles without this kind of protection. Similarly, in both Australia and Canada, local 'contact rules' restricting the amount of overseas content in radio broadcasting helped to preserve and foster local talent. In Canada's case, while its French-language stations (mimicking those of France itself) were clearly trying to preserve Francophone Canada as a cultural space, the country's English-language stations were just as clearly attempting to foster the development of local musicians. Similar strategies to promote local music (though with fewer strictures about language than those in France and Canada) were adopted in Sweden, which has arguably punched above its weight in world popular music since the 1970s triumphs of ABBA thanks to these regulations.

Such regulations, whatever their effects on the market, did not mean the preservation in aspic of performing styles. Scandinavian and Finnish death metal, Italian or Romanian progressive rock, Polish punk rock, and French, Italian and German-Turkish rap were each derived from Anglo-American forms, but were developed with local distinctiveness to address and sell within distinct local markets. Globalisation spoke with many languages and many more accents. And yet it remained globalisation. Despite the importance of music within local cultures (which can be serviced by recording), the marketing of 'world music' even on dedicated and enthusiastic specialist labels such as GlobeStyle promoted a Westernised sense of what music was. They divorced sound from its traditional context in exactly the way radio broadcasting and recording had done to Western opera, religious or dance music: in each case what had been music for popular rituals or audio-visual entertainments became music for 'the listener'. Similarly, through aspects of the folk roots movement, and of festivals such as WOMAD (World of Music and Dance), the Westernisation of world musical practices can be traced through collaborative, hybrid projects such as Afro Celt Sound System, which remove sonic information from its local-cultural context and/or tradition, and place it instead within that of product innovation and customer development.

So while the mutual exploration and discovery of musics from outside Europe and North America has been important to the development of the musical commodity, it has necessarily removed music from its place of origin, placing it before an audience moved by an aestheticised, and occasionally political, interest in 'the Other' as the repository of an imagined authenticity which has been lost to the industrialised and secularised West. This was the place of jazz in France and Scandinavia in the 1930s, or of Bulgarian choral music in late 1980s Western Europe as the Cold War ended and 'world music' became fashionable. However, these narrow aesthetic, political, ethnographic or archaeological tendencies became dissipated because by the end of the century world cities such as Paris, New York and London were not unicultural, or indeed in any obvious sense national, but were instead home to shifting and diverse populations each of which had some tendency to hybridise (and therefore the unanswerable question arose: Other than what?). Thanks to broadcasting and recording, musics no longer belonged solely to specific ethnic or political groups. By making music from everywhere available almost everywhere else in the world, the twentieth century's technologies put an end to such cultural secrets. The fluid boundaries among linguistic and political groups in large cities offered space for development of new forms and/or new markets, as for example the 1980s revival in New York of Klezmer, an Eastern European Jewish popular form touched by the other folk musics of Eastern Europe – and in its turn touching new performers in different genres, such as the African-American jazz clarinettist Don Byron.

Music and broadcasting: from prescription to plenitude

The growth of exposure to a wide variety of musics, and their subsequent development and hybridisation, is due in part to broadcasting. The technologies of radio spread widely in the 1920s, and by the 1930s broadcasting was a major element of communication and education, though it developed very differently in different parts of the world. In the USA the early established networks, two owned by NBC and one by CBS, helped radio to become an important national binding medium in the 1930s and especially during the Second World War. After the war, however, television began to replace radio as the dominant news and information service. By the mid-1950s some people were predicting the 'death of radio', but the medium reinvented itself as a provider of music and entertainment, interspersed with concentrated news and weather bulletins, and began to provide traffic news; in this form it became increasingly popular among car drivers, and users of portable transistor radios (or 'trannies' as they were affectionately called in the UK in the 1960s).

In the 1970s FM radio, which has better sound quality but more limited range than AM broadcasting, began its life span; this encouraged the multiplication of local stations in the United States (and Canada). Among these are the 1,500 or so American National Public Radio stations which were incorporated in the 1967 Public Broadcasting Act. However, while the number of local stations has increased massively, in fact commercial radio has increasingly been subject to the concentration of ownership. Most of the nearly 12,000 commercial AM and FM radio stations in the United States are apparently absolutely local, with local offices, and seem locally based in their music format (with country music stations in the Midwest, and 'urban contemporary' – i.e. black music – in the big cities) as well as their news and weather coverage. Almost all are in fact owned either by CBS Radio, or by Clear Channel Communications (an increasingly global corporation which also owns a number of UK entertainment companies, including the Mean Fiddler organisation which has run the Glastonbury festival since 2002). Quite apart from the question of ownership, most of these apparently local stations are in fact closely controlled nationally. Each company uses central computer-controlled sequencing to service the station's chosen format. Clear Channel also employs what have been called 'cyber-jocks'. Through a technology known as voice-tracking, DJs and continuity announcers can in fact service local stations from studios in major cities.

The last twenty years have seen a number of 'format' changes at American (and Canadian) FM stations. Formats such as Country, AOR, Urban Contemporary, and 'oldies', have been changed according to local market research, and/or broader shifts in taste or fashion. An early twenty-first century innovation indicates how radio is now in thrall to the digital age. The 'Jack FM' format incorporates all mainstream popular music from the mid-1960s, with some current chart singles. The format started as an internet webstream radio station, which, like all subsequent Jack FM stations, used the slogan 'playing what we want'. Thanks to this attitude Jack FM stations promote themselves as having larger and more varied playlists than other commercial radio – which they do: it is not unusual for a Jack-FM station to have a playlist of over 1,000 songs compared to normal FM stations which sometimes have playlists of fewer than 100 songs. Listeners sometimes refer to these stations as 'random radio' or as 'iPod shuffle radio'. Not everyone intends the comparison to be flattering. One of the main criticisms of the Jack FM format has been that thanks to the elimination (or at least reduction) of the role of the DJ, radio is actually losing its main selling point over an iPod in shuffle mode, which is the sense – often as it happens entirely erroneous – that a live person is programming your music.

The medium of radio developed very differently in Europe because of the different role of the State, which tended to grant monopolies over broadcasting. Radio in France and the UK, for example, follows a very similar developmental pattern. From the 1920s to the 1980s Radio France was the monopoly provider of radio. In 1965 its output was modernised into three channels providing news, light entertainment and high culture. By this time there were a number of commercial channels and pirate stations broadcasting, in French, into France from outside its borders, and in the 1980s, following pressure from the independent and commercial radio lobbies and pirate broadcasters, President Mitterrand allowed the licensing of the so-called 'radios libres', the first local stations outside the remit of Radio France. Initially provided with a state subsidy and then financed by commercial advertising, by 1986 these were grouped together into national commercial networks. In 2000, in response to their increasingly effective competition Radio France reorganised its radio network. France Bleu became a regional network, primarily on FM (the national AM radio network was recast as an information service) and several local stations based in large cities were closed down and replaced with the youth station Le Mouv'.

In the UK, the BBC (British Broadcasting Corporation) was set up in 1922 as a limited company, and in 1927 it was incorporated by a Royal Charter, with a then monopoly over public broadcasting. Instead of relying on advertising revenue, the organisation was forbidden to advertise, and it was funded by a compulsory broadcast licence, a tax which was paid by any UK resident who wished to receive programmes (it still is). The BBC was always acutely aware of its educational mission, and its music policy always included a great deal of classical music, including the commissioning of new music from leading British classical composers such as Edward Elgar and, later in the century, Benjamin Britten. The annual Proms concert festival, then heading for oblivion, was taken on by the BBC in 1927, and the BBC Symphony Orchestra was founded in 1930 partly in order to become the festival's house orchestra. Each has been subsidised by the licence payer ever since.

All this support of classical music was based on a belief that this form of music was simply the best, and that it was the BBC's role to lead public taste until everyone else agreed. The BBC's first director general, Lord Reith, was convinced that broadcasting 'must not be for entertainment purposes alone'. However from the start the corporation did broadcast light music – live relays of dances from hotel ballrooms, with music provided by stalwarts such as Ted Heath's big band, were a regular feature – and during the Second World War there was a quantum leap in the amount of 'light music' broadcast by the BBC.

It was recognised that the provision of entertaining music would help the war effort, and indeed while programmes such as 'Music While You Work' embodied this severely functional attitude, there was also a great deal of after-work and weekend music and musical comedy starting with 'Friday Night is Music Night': concerts by popular singers, big bands and brass bands, and records introduced by friendly DJs. After the war this type of programming was organised into a dedicated channel, the Light Programme, while the Home Service provided news and the Third Programme high culture. In 1967 the Light Programme was repackaged as Radio Two, while at the same time the corporation belatedly launched a pop music channel, Radio One, and another repackaged channel, Radio Three, was reserved for classical music and occasionally equally serious drama.

Radio One had come into being because of competition from 'pirate' commercial stations (the best known being Radio Caroline, which was quite literally a 'pirate', with its studio and radio equipment in a small ship anchored just outside British territorial waters). Caroline broadcast 24-hour pop and therefore attracted the teenage and young adult consumers that advertisers most wanted to reach. Because of these commercial possibilities the pirates were backed by the commercial interests of the City of London, and especially the record labels, who wanted the opportunity to sell to young people via advertising. Radio One was a compromise. It was not at first a 24-hour station, and thanks to pressure from the Musicians' Union to preserve jobs for live performers, it did not play records all day. Sound quality was poor as the waveband allocated was a particularly noisy part of the AM spectrum. But though it did not directly advertise, it did some of what the City wanted: the station was in effect a showcase for the products of the music industry, which were played in rotation according to the formulaic scheme known as a 'playlist' which featured a set number of new releases, established chart hits and classic tracks every hour.

Subsequent developments in BBC radio have usually been driven by outside pressures rather than by innovative programme makers or enlightened management policy. In the 1970s the BBC's monopoly was challenged by the introduction of commercial local radio stations such as Capital FM; in the 1980s licences were sold for national as well as local stations, and dedicated jazz, rock and dance music stations appeared; but so did new pirate radio stations, broadcasting some or all of the more extreme dance music, and/or the African-American, Caribbean and South Asian musics which the BBC and the new commercial stations continued to neglect. In the mid-1990s Radio One adopted a policy of appealing to listeners under 25 (and immediately lost two thirds of its audience, most of which had been with it since 1967), and in consequence Radio Two began to programme more old pop hits and Adult-Oriented Rock; its audience increased substantially. There was still not enough black music, British or otherwise, on either station, and early in the new millennium the arrival of Digital Audio Broadcasting (DAB) digital radio led to the launch of new BBC channels dedicated to black music (1xtra), as well as to rock and older pop (Radio 6).

DAB is a technological specification which was designed in the late 1980s and pioneered in parts of the UK a decade later, with national coverage due to be complete by the end of 2007. The UK has paid the usual penalty for being an 'early adopter' of digital radio: DAB technology has not delivered on all its promises. The original objectives included claims that digital radio would enable higher fidelity, lower noise, more reliable mobile services such as car radio, and many new services which would enable the broadcasting of archive material and the targeting of ethnic minorities.

These new services have indeed been offered – at the time of writing there are some 50 DAB digital radio stations available in the London area alone. But this new variety of choice is part of the problem. Listeners to the UK's DAB radio offerings quickly, and crossly, agreed that the service invariably offered audio quality significantly lower than that available on FM. The broadcasters were accused of sacrificing audio quality in favour of squeezing in additional services on the multiplexes which carry the signal. There is a fundamental technical problem because of the ways in which the signal is encoded and decoded, and it is unlikely to be solved without significant expansion of available bandwidth; in simple terms this means that the amount of digital information output per station is too low to achieve the sound quality already available on FM. Having noted these problems, Sweden and Holland are among the countries which have halted plans to roll out DAB in the hope that a cheaper system with higher quality audio output will emerge, and at the time of writing the USA and Japan were trialling different digital radio technologies.

But new technologies such as DAB, and cultural innovations such as the Jack radio station format, are not the only examples of the ambivalent impact of the digital world on radio broadcasting. Arguably the most important computers associated with radio are the machines which are responsible simultaneously for the scheduling of playlists and the payment and collection of royalties. Many people believe that disc jockeys at radio stations are responsible for choosing the music which is heard on their shows. In reality, playlists for the entire day have usually been generated *a priori* by someone using a computerised music scheduling system. Music scheduling systems search databases of the songs in active rotation at a radio station, and choose from them according to a set of 'rules' for sequencing them in accordance with specific stations' music broadcasting policies. Most radio station 'formats' will have strict, and different, rules about the number of contemporary chart hits, new releases or classic tracks which can be played in any one hour or on any one DJ's show on subsequent days. There are also rules for what kinds of songs may succeed another according to length, tempo, gender of vocalist(s) or other characteristics.

Meanwhile the internet has become a major resource for the streaming of audio materials, and this means radio broadcasting among other things. Even radio which is not actually digitally broadcast on FM or AM can be digitised for internet streaming, and through this means, even local radio stations addressing small populations through low-power transmitters can achieve a global audience. Real-time transmission then raises a problem of reception across time boundaries, and there are a number of ways in which such global time problems can be offset. Many stations now also offer 'podcasts' of shows recorded in MP3 format, which can be downloaded automatically to computers or MP3 players and heard in the listener's own time, while a number of software programmes such as *Hit-Recorder* also offer the possibility of recording the music output of one or more stations to a computer's hard drive.

As well as encouraging the wider reach of existing radio stations, the internet has encouraged the further growth of internet-only micro-radio stations which a generation ago might have functioned as illegal local 'pirate' stations. Playlisting – from the posting of lists on MySpace to their repeated playing – has emerged as a way in which individuals can make a personal stamp on the web, somewhat akin to 'blogging', though the results of this form of display are not always strictly personal – the Amazon internet shopping website, for example, will display users' playlists when it detects that a searcher is interested in these users' tastes, all in the hope of encouraging more consumption, of course. The resulting excess of choice has exerted pressure on established providers of radio services – the emergent Jack format among them – especially as the smaller internet stations are less likely to interrupt the music flow by adverts.

All these new formats, from the major broadcasters' output streamed on the internet at the same time as the scheduled programme is transmitted by orthodox means, to the micro-station's playlist, raise very serious issues concerning the ownership of music, and the payment of rights and royalties to those owners. Models of payment for composers, performers, record labels and publishers which have evolved for land-based radio stations have had to be rethought in order to deal with the new radio services: this is macro-broadcasting, across national boundaries, to micro-audiences. This rethinking occurs as the music business is at its most defensive, faced by falling CD sales, systematic CD piracy and the rise of internet file-sharing, and also in some territories falling audiences for conventional radio stations. The owners of the new digital stations, meanwhile, are naturally concerned to keep their own cost base low; their advertisers (if any) are unlikely to pay at the same rate as they do for mass-broadcast stations. The new radio stations are therefore unwilling to subscribe to a payment model which does not reflect their small audience base.

Television has to face a similar problem. Rock'n'roll and mass television emerged at the same moment, the mid-1950s. In helping to broadcast it around the world, television played an important part in the new music's evolution as well as its diffusion. Until the advent of MTV, however, television did not serve popular music particularly well. This was partly for technological reasons: until the 1980s television loudspeakers produced poor quality mono sound, which like the soundtrack mix itself was usually tailored for the spoken voice, and therefore deficient in bass response. But there were also programming issues. In the era before multi-channel television could identify and address niche audiences, music programming was made to fit with the general demands of the schedule, which was for the largest audience possible: family entertainment.

In order to fulfil this function, American 'music' shows such as *The Monkees* and *The Partridge Family* were through-scripted narrative dramas in which musical performances played a modest role. Other American shows featured musicians such as Pat Boone, Sonny and Cher, the Carpenters and Andy Williams acting as hosts for shows in a 'variety' format which was an extension of vaudeville, aimed at a domestic family audience, rather than the soul and rock musics which were developing a different concert tradition with its own dedicated and strongly age-related public. Music with a harder edge was confined to a few specialist shows such as *Soul Train*, which first aired in 1971 and became the first black American music show to achieve widespread syndication in the USA, or the BBC's long-running, strangely named live-performance show *The Old Grey Whistle Test*, which first aired in the same year and lasted in one form or another until 1987. The BBC's chart show, *Top of the Pops*, first appeared in 1964, and survived various corporate attempts to kill it off for over forty years, broadcasting weekly until its final closure in mid-2006.

Nonetheless even in its early family-entertainment stage, television was a vital showcase for musicians. Two of the best-known acts in popular music made good use of television to launch and relaunch aspects of their careers, despite television's over-anxious use of their talents. Elvis Presley appeared twice on the Steve Allen show in 1956; thanks to public concern about his appearance and body movements, on the second occasion, groomed to reassure and dressed in a tuxedo, he stood still and sang his hit version of the Lieber and Stoller song 'Hound Dog' – to a bassett hound, which sat dutifully before him. Notoriously, on an appearance on the Ed Sullivan Show in the following year, a less formally dressed Elvis was shown only from the waist up. In each case the show's producers had decided that the singer's hip movements would be too inflammatory for a family audience; needless to say the resulting publicity did his career the world of good. In 1968 Presley made a television special which, aired on NBC in December, successfully relaunched his career as a singer after a decade in which he had made a number of very indifferent films and music had taken second place. Similarly the Beatles' (far less controversial) first appearances on the Ed Sullivan show in 1964 helped to cement their early success in the USA. When, in 1967, they gave up touring and became a studio band, one of the first results was their own television special, the strange (and subsequently somewhat neglected) *Magical Mystery Tour*. But these are indeed examples of top-line acts, and therefore unusual; though there were half-hour pop shows on most European countries by the early 1960s, this was nothing like enough airtime. Most musicians simply did not have the opportunity to be seen on television, let alone to dominate the television schedules.

All this began to change in the early 1980s; since 1981, in fact, popular music all over the world has become increasingly audio-visual. At this point MTV was introduced in the USA as the world's first music television channel; it quickly achieved exposure in non-Communist Europe and Asia. In its early years the channel provided a constant diet of promotional videos, with continuity provided by the equivalent of the disc jockey, the video-jockey or V-J. If in its early years this was globalisation of the crudest kind, offering an eager public mainly white Anglo-American rock and pop recorded by major labels, the channel has subsequently expanded worldwide both in diversity of content and in geographical focus, with separate channels broadcasting a different mix of content into the UK, southern and mid-Europe, Scandinavia, Latin America, the Asia-Pacific and so on; there are also separate United States-based MTV channels aimed at Chinese-Americans and South-Asian-Americans. (There is also a comprehensive and rapidly developing website which can access all these and more.)

Moving popular music to its own channel was in one sense 'good' for music on television. Now music was not just a part of the general flow of television, alongside news, soaps, sports programmes and advertisements, but wall-to-wall (and subsequently mall-to-mall). In the early days of the format, music companies provided their promotional videos free to the MTV channel; this benefited all sides, with free promotion for the musicians involved. But it was not greatly to the benefit of musical diversity. Videos added greatly to the recording costs of any band or singer, and companies began to spend significant sums of money on directors, producers, sets and film crews at the expense of the number and range of musicians they signed and albums they released; broadcasters and record labels alike agreed that as this was a form of promotion, they would refuse to pay performer royalties to musicians when the videos were broadcast. However, when cash flow became tight in the economic recession at the beginning of the 1990s, music companies began to charge music television channels for their material, arguing fairly reasonably that they had been providing free programming for an increasingly profitable organisation. The MTV group responded by diversifying its offering, commissioning some non-music programming, and moving some of its channels away from the wall-to-wall video approach.

23

The MTV formula has also been broadened because it has lost its USP – the number of channels offering music video increased (including a number under the MTV company, but also a number of other channels such as *Kerrang!* and *Smash Hits*). MTV itself has sought to maintain a market-leading position by providing the best product for the late teenage/young-adult consumer. This has meant principally the development of a laddish 'MTV culture' in commissioning programmes ranging from the still music-video-based *Beavis and Butthead* to the comedic self-abuse of *Jackass*, in which the activities shown have little or nothing to do with music (though there's often a pumping soundtrack playing while the people involved make fools of themselves). This shift is in effect a recolonising of 'ordinary' rather than music television, a new kind of variety show made and watched by people used to extreme sports and reality television alike, and who share a slacker/skater ideology which sees young-adult masculinity without responsibilities as the apex of civilisation. The MTV2 channel, for example, was described promotionally as 'the irreverent brother MTV never knew it had', while MTV's Flux channel builds on this sense of a culture in common by encouraging viewer participation through onscreen internet and mobile phone messaging, submitted video and increased choice of programming. The advent of this user-led programming in what had once been to all intents and purposes 'music-*industry* television' leads to an important point about the changing nature of the ways in which music is used in contemporary society. Less music is broadcast as a thing in itself, and more as part of something else, whether that something is a 'promotional' video, a computer game, or a television or film soundtrack. Much more than merely reflecting this change, MTV has helped to bring it about.

The proliferation of music channels through television (and increasingly also through the internet) is another aspect of the digital culture. They appear to offer a wider range of choice, and through modes of recording such as Sky Plus, Tivo, and website replay, also offer increasingly efficient ways of accessing the programmes when the viewer actually wishes to see them. At the time of writing Sky Digital television offered twenty-one music channels and sixty radio channels for the UK subscriber with plenty of time on their hands, but – as with the analogue multi-channel television in the USA condemned so eloquently and accurately in Bruce Springsteen's song '57 channels and nothing on' – coverage was limited to a few formats: chart pop, adult rock, r'n'b and rap, and the lighter end of metal.

The activity of 'listening' to music on television has benefited hugely from technical developments in the delivery of television sound itself, such as Nicam stereo and the Dolby 5.1 surround-sound system which was pioneered in cinemas and has become fairly routine in the home since the 1990s. These innovations, and the rapid growth of DVD sales, have led to a massive increase in the quality of cinema and television sound, and though there has been an increase in interest in (and sales of) film and TV soundtrack albums, there has also been a far more significant increase in the purchase and use of high-quality audio-visual material for the domestic environment. Nonetheless the success of the new audio-visual formats (and the proliferation of music-television channels) have led to the new commercial sales category of 'DVD music' – though this is principally another form of recycling, as it involves firstly, retrospective compilations of promotional videos such as Madonna's *Immaculate Collection* (Warner 1999); secondly, a great deal of archival release of concerts and recording studio footage such as *Frank Sinatra: Concert for the Americas* (a 1982 concert released on Warner in 2002); thirdly, discussions of the 'making of' classic albums such as *Queen – the Making of A Night at the Opera* (Eagle Rock Entertainment 2006); fourthly, recordings of live gigs using familiar material, such as *What We Did Last Summer: Robbie Williams Live at Knebworth* (EMI 2003); and fifthly, classic rock and soul albums or concerts with original mono or stereo soundtracks remixed for 5.1 surround sound, such as the *Cream Farewell Concert* (a 1968 event originally recorded for television and re-released on Sony BMG in 2001).

Nostalgia purchasing, in other words, has become a key aspect of the selling of music. There's nothing here which is culturally specific to the digital age. Even before the introduction of the CD format, 'classic' rock was being repackaged for the older collector with more money to spend and worn-out vinyl to replace. But the launch of CD itself – the first digital format – led to a mass repackaging of material which had first appeared on vinyl and/or cassette. Many people, convinced of the reliability as well as the improved sound quality of the new format, were persuaded to buy transferred, remastered versions of albums they already owned. By the early years of the new millennium, UK market researchers had characterised such purchasers as 'fifty quid bloke', a man in his thirties or older who thought nothing of spending fifty pounds or more on music every time he entered a store, while younger people might be more careful with money, and/or might be more interested in downloading music, for free if possible, than in buying hard copies on CD.

The young, in other words, have grown up during the increasing use of the personal computer as an entertainment centre. In the 1980s, computers became useful tools for music composition and sampling – and games playing. This form of audiovisual entertainment has produced another new music category, computer games with composed soundtracks. Arcade games in the 1970s contained primitive sound-generating facilities which were largely dedicated to providing a satisfying swish of white noise to accompany the player's extermination of an unfortunate alien invader. As games machines used faster processing speeds, so their sound-generating capabilities improved, and composers began to become involved, firstly in programming repetitive fragments which accompanied the player's moves. However soundtracks for games remained a relatively unimportant, and underdeveloped, part of the entertainment until the 1990s, when the common appearance of sound cards for personal computers such as the Creative Soundblaster series introduced a step change in sound quality for video games (and more generally in music replayed on PCs). Whether sampled or synthesised, orchestral and hard rock sounds were now available for game soundtracks, and subsequently some games have commissioned soundtracks by composers active in other fields of music.

Trent Reznor's score for *Quake* is a relatively well-known example of this emergent genre, while arguably the hardest-working composer for video games is Japanese composer Nobuo Oematsu. A self-taught musician, Oematsu has composed in rock, techno and classical orchestral modes for games such as the *Final Fantasy* series. His music has been among the leading lights in a series of orchestral concerts featuring games music which started in Tokyo in 1991; the first such venture outside Japan took place in the German city of Liepzig in 2003 (as part of the Liepzig Computer Games Conference), and has subsequently been repeated in other parts of the world.

The orchestras involved in these projects are not alone in their attempts to bring video-game music out of the gamer's bedroom and into the concert hall: there are video-game tribute bands in (at least) Canada, the USA, Denmark, and Finland. To take two complementary examples, the Brazilian band MegaDriver credit themselves as the inventors of 'game metal' – as their name implies, they play (only) metal versions of the scores for games written for the Sega MegaDrive; and similarly Daniel Brown's *Nintendo on Piano* website does precisely what it says, offering recordings of his performances, and also sheet music transcriptions for the consumer to play, of the music for a great many Nintendo games.

Since the early 1990s, the World Wide Web has facilitated the uploading and sharing of sound (and images), and increases in memory and storage capacity and the development of file-compression formats such as MP3 have made it easier to store files containing music and moving images. Personal computers have therefore become adjuncts to the entertainment industry, able to play and store games, films and music (and pornography, which is still widely regarded as the internet's most profitable sector) with relatively high-quality sound and image reproduction, and to facilitate instant shared responses to the entertainment through chat rooms and fan sites. We should remember that in many homes the computer is present in children's bedrooms as well as the family living or work space; it can therefore form part of a non-parental culture. There would have been no Napster without the PC and internet – and (illegal) P2P file sharing in general would probably not have taken off without the relatively private access to a PC which a bedroom affords. There would have been no iPod without the Mac or PC as partner – indeed most portable MP3 players have to have a relationship with a host computer.

The key twenty-first century development in the selling of commercial entertainment material has also had a huge impact on the ways in which we conceptualise the local. This is the introduction of audio-visual content for portable players and mobile communications devices. Perhaps *despite* the success of audio-only MP3 players such as the original iPod, (and the relative failure of the original Sony portable television the 'watchman' introduced in 1984, which has only been a niche market product ever since), what is increasingly offered for portable players is not just music as such but, again, audio-visual entertainment of which music is an important component. The 'iPod video' player, in appearance the same as its predecessor the 60GB photo iPod (which as the name suggests could already store and display photos as well as playing music files), was launched in the autumn of 2005, and subsequent Apple plans included a number of other audio-visual devices including the iPhone. While the iPod video player offers the user the opportunity to download and store music videos alongside music files and podcasts of spoken-word material such as radio broadcasts, many companies now offer audiovisual vodcasts or streaming 'live' 'television' news, sports and music channels (such as MTV), and other audio-visual content specifically for mobile phones as well as for PCs. At the time of writing, this apparent utopia of live audio-visual entertainment for small hand-held devices was in fact far from fully realised. A number of problems concerning digital rights management, the ownership of (and methods of payment for) content, and the desire among service providers and mobile phone networks to offer exclusivity, meant that the user's choices of content were effectively limited, and consequently take-up of the new services was relatively low.

Whatever the general interest surrounding these innovations, the potential future uses of mobile technology might not, then, be fully realised in the ways that the industry wants. But the positive hype over mobile audiovisual content (which is of moderate broadcast quality at best), and the gradual increase in take-up, should be contrasted with the apparent failure so far of the most recent, relatively unhyped, and comparatively old-style, innovations in hi-fi music format. These are the so-called 'super-audio' formats such as High Definition CD (HDCD), Super Audio CD (SACD), and DVD-Audio (DVD-A), which began to appear in 2000. These formats each offer a far higher technical specification than audio CD. More information can be recorded, so frequency response and dynamic range can be wider, and music can be mixed for and decoded in multi-channel, multi-speaker surround sound. In the case of DVD-A, significantly more material can be put on one disc. However, the new **27** formats are mutually incompatible, and in each case dedicated players are needed with dedicated chips to decode their multi-channel sound and visual/textual extras. Though some specialist hi-fi companies have invested considerable sums in developing dedicated players for them (including a few play-all models which incorporate decoders for each of the formats), it is thought at the time of writing that these formats will no longer be supported by the mainstream recording companies after the first decade of the century.

Writing from early 2007, it is worth noting the existing 'generic failure' of these audio-only ultra-high-fidelity formats, which may only survive through relatively small-scale labels selling classical or jazz recordings. Though the major record labels have yet again remixed and repackaged a few old favourites for the middle-aged re-buyer in the new ultra-hi-fi, such as Pink Floyd's *Dark Side of the Moon* and the Beach Boys' *Pet Sounds*, and though there's a fair amount of new mainstream rock and pop, there's little or no *new* alternative rock, punk, folk, jazz or country in the super-audio formats.

The relative failure so far of the super-audio discs would seem to indicate that too few people are prepared to pay significant sums of money in order to experience what they perceive as a relatively small increase in the quality of recorded sound. As well as having to buy new players, the user must purchase discs which are more expensive than a conventional CD – and CDs were already far too expensive in the view of everyone but the record companies. What they then get has a number of technical problems, thanks to the inexact nature of the specification for the formats, which might range from a lack of delay control (which is very useful in large rooms with multi-speaker systems) to a worrying range of digital rights management (DRM) programmes both in the players and on the discs. DRM devices are designed to prevent copying but according to some users actually interfere with the greater resolution potentially offered by the formats. For example, thanks to this anxiety about copying, though it is advertised as a high-end *digital* format, DVD-Audio will not actually output all its information digitally. Its digital output is in PCM stereo; only the analogue audio outputs on DVD-A players will give the listener the full benefit of unprocessed separate-channel surround-sound.

Anyway, as carriers of music, to most listeners the new super-audio provided an answer to a question no-one was asking. Many listeners insist that the audio CD was and is for almost all purposes a good enough format for concentrated domestic listening. MP3 players, on the other hand – which even at their best offer sound of significantly lower quality than the CDs which they encode – have been successful because they are convenient: they can be made very small while storing a great deal of information, and are therefore well adapted for personal use; they are in this sense the direct inheritors of the audio cassette Walkman, which similarly sold very well despite using the comparatively lo-fi cassette format.

Perhaps, then, the story of the evolution of listening in the early years of the new century could be couched in terms of a continuing individualisation of consumer audio, in which the personal soundworld of the Walkman and its younger MP3 relatives has gradually gained ground over the more easily shared soundworlds available through orthodox domestic hi-fi. If so we have to qualify such an assertion both virtually and literally. In the virtual world, the MP3 file has led to a newly networked sense of the sharing of musical taste, largely through the explosion in illegal file-sharing. Back in the 'real' world, the MP3 file has become a hi-fi object. Specialist manufacturers offer a number of hard-drive based players which store MP3 files and interface between computer and hi-fi amplifiers and speakers, while British hi-fi manufacturers Arcam and Naim Audio each offered a dedicated iPod input into fairly expensive hi-fi receiver equipment which was launched in 2005. For users of any of these devices public and private soundworlds, and the quality trade-offs of the personal listening device, have blurred.

These synergies (and trade-offs with sound quality) are already common in the ways in which musical entertainment is presented in that most important public/private arena, the car. The car radio was the first portable music technology, able to provide the listener with a tailored sonic environment (a set of choices which multiplied with the arrival of in-car 8-track tape and stereo cassette players in the early 1970s) but the obvious limits of the car meant that the development of a truly portable, play-anywhere sound environment was taken on in increasingly small portable radios. The first 'pocket-sized' radio was introduced by Sony in 1957. Sony was also responsible for arguably the biggest-ever step in personal entertainment for public space, the audio cassette Walkman, which was introduced in 1979. Sony chairman Akio Morita championed this device, a small cassette player with headphones, insisting that it should be marketed as a mass product rather than an expensive executive toy. From the start therefore the Sony Walkman was advertised and priced to appeal to young people; the product range was subsequently developed to include models with radios and recording facilities, and by the end of the 1990s sales by Sony alone had exceeded 250 million worldwide (most other Japanese electronics manufacturers offered very similar devices, though the name Walkman remained a Sony trademark, and the name everyone used, whatever the other manufacturers actually called their models). The success of the Walkman format (and of in-car cassette players) meant far greater sales for both blank and pre-recorded cassettes; it meant that music consumers thought about what music suited their mobile players, and the travel compilation tape became an important part of many music users' collections.

The portable CD player was launched in the early days of the new format, the early 1980s, and soon became similarly ubiquitous; again, in-car CD players were also quickly available. During the 1990s the increasing use of blank recordable CDs, hi-fi CD recorders, and CD burners on personal computers, meant that users' compilations remained an important part of portable music. As with the personal compilation on audio cassette, users were challenging the hegemony of 'the album' as manufactured by the major record labels, and choosing only the material they liked, in the order they liked. Such choices importantly prefigure the arrival of the personal MP3 player and the era of the playlist.

The first portable MP3 player was the Diamond Multimedia Systems Rio PMP 300, which was introduced in the USA in 1998. This small hand-held unit could store one hour's worth of music, and the device came with a software programme to be used in the user's computer, and a cable for connecting the Rio to the computer. The software converted CD recordings (or other sound files) in the standard, memory-hungry WAV format to much smaller MP3 files. Though the record industry soon tried to ban both the player and software on the grounds that their copyrights were bound to be infringed, the American courts denied their request (this was just before the Napster phenomenon took off and music-business lobbying against personal digital technology reached fever pitch). A number of electronics and computer companies then began to develop similar portable players which would download music files stored on personal computers. One such company was Apple, which set up an engineering team led by Tony Fadell to develop a device based on a design specification from a Silicon Valley company called Portal Player (who had also tried to sell their ideas to Sony). The result was a device which had an internal 5GB hard drive which could store about 66 hours of music, so it enjoyed a far bigger storage capacity than the Rio player. It was cigarette-pack small with very simple good looks, including a moulded white plastic front bonded to a metal casing back, and very chic in-ear headphones on instantly recognisable trademark white leads. It had a clear screen with a relatively easy user interface, and it operated in relationship both with a host computer and also – if the user wished – with an online music store which could download tracks to the computer and thence to the new device. The internet Portable Database, or iPod.

MP3 culture: pleasure and anxiety

The iconic personal music device of the new millennium was launched at precisely the right time, towards the end of 2001. Thanks to the success of Napster software, at this point people were used to the idea that they could download songs and store them on their computers. Thanks to the increasing recording-industry backlash *against* Napster and its users, the industry wanted desperately to find and support a site for the legal, paid-for downloading of music, which is why Apple were able to set up iTunes on what the recording industry has subsequently claimed were very favourable terms. This in turn meant that Apple was able to offer music for a small enough sum (99 US cents per track in the USA, 79p in the UK and 99 euro cents in Europe at the time of launch) actually to tempt those people who were angry that the record industry charged rip-off prices for CDs, but who did not want to criminalise themselves by downloading music illegally, into buying music online.

The iPod has generated a substantial literary culture of its own, including a number of celebratory publications such as magazine editor Dylan Jones's occasionally thoughtful book *iPod, therefore I am*. However, most of the many books on the iPod are not so much celebrations but (celebratory) users' guides – with titles such as *iPod and iTunes for Dummies; Absolute Beginners Guide to iPod and iTunes; The iPod: All You Need to Know;* and *The Art of Downloading Music* (which is chiefly about the iPod, but unlike most of these books acknowledges that there are other MP3 players out there). This would seem to indicate either that the manufacturer's own user guides are inadequate; or that they have hidden some of the ways in which the equipment can be used; or that the books' publishers and authors at least assume that the mass of the population is less technically literate than the designers of computer equipment would like them to be. There is even, it seems, a fear that the lack of ability to use new high-technology devices has inhibited their uptake. In 2005 upmarket London store Selfridges was offering tuition for iPod beginners, at £65 for forty minutes.

This anxiety is part of a much wider concern with 'media literacy' (which I refer to at more length in chapter five). Concern about people's lack of technical competence probably started in the early 1980s, when some users admitted that they could not programme their own video recorders. In the age of increasingly interactive multi-channel television and radio, of multi-channel and multi-speaker hi-fi, and of convergence between all these and computers, consumers do have to know rather more about their equipment than how to press the 'on' switch, or to remember where they left the remote control.

Of course there *are* many proficient and enthusiastic users who have adopted (and adapted) the device to their own ends: this innovative use, rather than the plethora of style and how-to books, is the heart of the 'cult' of the iPod. For example, MP3 files of 'mash-ups' (home-made mixes which combine two or more existing commercial songs) are put on websites for general sharing – much to the annoyance of the record companies involved in the original recordings, who spend a great deal of money, time and effort closing down such websites and/or warning people not to play the mixes. In the words of Tamar Newton, a contributor to an iPod-DJ user website:

> Mash-ups are the perfect soundtrack for the iPod generation where everyone is permanently switched on to their own personal soundtrack. It's to feel a sense of immediate exciting schizophrenia, perusing the cheese counter with your little white ear-plugs screaming twenty-seven different songs into your head at once. With different backing tracks.[2]

Slightly less controversially, iPod playlists are swapped and rated on websites, and have even been used on some American university campus websites for 'playlist dating', in which, it seems, students try to attract sexual partners by displaying the size of their, er… music collections. iPod-DJs perform at parties, either using ordinary mixers or dedicated multi-iPod hardware which – like the Arcam and Naim hi-fi equipment – helps to change this highly personal musical device into a public musical instrument, by using the individual iPod as if it were a turntable.

For many users, however, the most important adapted use of the iPod (or any other MP3 player) is not music but in podcasting – the downloading and storage of radio broadcasts, newspaper reports or other sound material for listening to when convenient. Like SMS text messaging on mobile phones, this was a use of the technology the industry did not foresee (though both broadcasters and Apple themselves soon catered for them – iPods soon began to list 'podcasts' on their index screens). More memory-hungry audio-visual 'vodcasts' are increasingly widely available. While there are many 'official' podcasts, and most radio stations and newspapers now offer some or all of their daily offering in podcast form, there are also a great many amateur web-based podcasters who use the format as an aural equivalent to blogging; and some who are in effect podcast-DJs, again using this variation on technological communication to broadcast their own musical taste.

The success story of the early iPods was dogged by a number of complaints over such matters as battery life and hard-disk unreliability, and increasingly over the machines' lack of inter-operability. Though the point of the design was that the case should always remain closed, with the assumption apparently being that if it ceased to work, the unit should be thrown away rather than serviced, Apple

---

2   www.ipod-dj.com/tamarjan05.html, accessed 14 November 2006

eventually agreed to replace batteries for the more disgruntled owners. More spectacularly, the introduction in 2005 of the ultraslim iPod Nano, launched with an expensive advertising campaign which focused on the unit's good looks rather than its utility as a music player, was not an unqualified success. Some users found that the screens – thinner than those on the larger devices – could be scratched, and even easily cracked. One of these unsatisfied customers, Matthew Peterson, annoyed at Apple's claims that the product had in fact been perfectly well prepared for market, set up a website, www.flawedmusicplayer.com. He invited fellow users to post pictures of the cracked screens on their own Nanos, and they did so in large numbers. Within a few days the manufacturer had compromised: the errant devices were being replaced, and Peterson agreed to close his website. However, while they insisted that there was no fundamental fault with the design of the product, Apple advised users to buy cases for their Nanos to protect the screens, and a group of users then launched a class action against Apple in the Californian courts claiming that in giving this advice Apple had admitted the screen was not suitable for purpose. Meanwhile Apple stock had dropped significantly – leading some shareholders to accuse Matthew Peterson of sabotaging their life savings.

Whatever the role played by the internet-connected public, there will be future devices with the same cultural impact as the iPod. Whether perfectly suited to the user or adaptable to unforeseen use, in a capitalist economic system all technology, always, is transitional. The search for continued profit means that models – whether cars, washing machines or music players – are constantly being upgraded and redeveloped; many devices are made obsolete even if they work perfectly well, in order to force the consumer to pay for something else which does more or less the same thing: the projected switch-off of analogue television and radio is a good example. Computerised devices are always examples of transitional technology, and the iPod is no different. At a point where connectability to the rest of the digital information world, and interoperability among different devices, are seen as the key parameters of any future successful product, by these criteria the iPod (and any other early-twenty-first century portable MP3 player) has a limited shelf-life. The audio cassette Walkman lasted about fifteen years, 1980–95, as a prime cultural and consumer form, and the CD Walkman likewise had a heyday of at best some fifteen years from 1985–2000. The first generation iPod and its variants, each of which relies on cable connection to a host computer and is without much PC functionality or direct dial-up connection to the internet, is likely to join the list of desirable items of retrotechnology well before the celebration of its first decade in 2011. No doubt its fully wireless 'replacement' will have an equally significant impact on the ways in which we think about and use music in the second decade of the new millennium.

The replacement device is highly likely to be similar to or a variant of the 'smartphones' currently at their early stages of development, which offer video and audio capabilities as well as an increasing range of computer functions – the iPhone is among the front runners here. When coupled with a hard drive or other mass storage facility, such devices will be able to challenge the hegemony of any communications and entertainment medium, whether it be a mobile or landline telephone, newspaper, radio, television, desktop or laptop PC, or an MP3 player.

Thanks to the successful diffusion of recording and broadcasting technologies up to and including MP3 players and smartphones, we now live in a world characterised by the availability of music in almost all genres almost everywhere, whether it is being relayed through public address systems in the shopping mall or on our own mobile music players or telephones. Most of the music ever recorded is available, and more is being released, mashed-up, remixed, file-shared and playlisted all the time. Where does all this saturated superfluity, easy availability, and multiple-choice of available sound files and playlists, sound carriers and personal soundworlds, leave 'music', how we think about it, and how we use it?

Chapter two

The changing places of music in the digital era: mobile, and immobile, sounds

The changes in the diffusion and availability of music have necessarily affected the ways in which we think about (as well as use) music as personal and/or public information. This chapter therefore explores music, identity and representation within our changing ideas of domestic and public space. These relationships have changed massively in recent times thanks to the appearance of generally affordable personal digital mobile communication devices (mobile phones, wireless laptop computers) and portable sound carriers (such as the iPod and other 'MP3 Walkman' devices) alongside orthodox hi-fi and other domestic sound carriers such as desktop computers; and thanks to the 'privatisation' of public spaces.

Music in domestic space

'Listening' to music, in other words hearing sonic information abstracted from the conditions of its production, was among the twentieth century's most characteristic practices – and it was a new experience. After the invention of recording, a new category of human experience, *listening* to music, appeared, and a new category of human subject, 'the listener', was created. For example, music journalist Dave Hill remembers the 1970s:

> There was this bloke and there was me and we really got along. Our friendship was founded on our mutual passions for pop music, indolence and substance abuse. We would sit around together, heroically stoned, and play records all day long: punk records, soul records, horny disco records like 'Hot Stuff' by Donna Summer....[3]

Dave Hill's friendship, which was built on the mutual exploration of music not through performance, or attendance at live concerts, but through listening to purchased recordings, is a deeply twentieth-century experience. It's worth remembering how far we are from the lost world of music before the development of recording. Before the invention of the gramophone at the end of the nineteenth century, 'music' was something you did yourself, individually or with others, or you persuaded or paid other people to do it in front of you, and it could only happen live, leaving no trace of its presence beyond the score

---

[3] Dave Hill, 'Doing What Comes Naturally', *The Independent Magazine*, 8 April 2000, p.32

(which was silent) or the memories of performers and listeners. Music in the home, or the church, or at the village dance (as well as the professional public entertainment of opera or the music hall), was also, always, made in real time by people who had learned the techniques of singing or playing instruments. The music business was at this point based around the publishing of sheet music for musicians, whether amateur or professional. For performer and audience alike, the only experience of music was as an immediate, audio-visual, live event.

But at the end of the nineteenth century music made by professional players and singers invaded the private space of the home through the new musical machines such as the player-piano and the gramophone. These devices provided for the first time a *record*, a repeatable trace of the same performance, something which was more accurate and immediate than memory. Record players were joined in the 1920s by radio, which offered both live music from outside the home, and also repeated traces of performances through the radio airplay of recordings.

The technologies of radio broadcasting and sound recording, in separating the listener from the musical practitioner, helped to create a new skill – that of listening without visual stimulus, even to music which had been written in order to be part of events which were seen as well as heard. After the mid-century, as the new technologies of long-playing records made it possible to record longer pieces of music without disruptive side changes, and at the same time innovations such as hi-fi (in the early 1950s) and stereo (in the later 1950s and early 1960s) improved sound quality, there was increasing demand for recordings not just of concert musics from symphonies to jazz, but of the music for audiovisual forms such as music for the Catholic Mass, film scores, musicals, opera and ballet. People now simply listened to operas and musicals which were written for the theatre; to church music which had been intended to have a ritual setting and spiritual meaning; and to dance musics which were meant for active participation rather than armchair appreciation (which in turn helped jazz to become concert music).

In order to enable the skill of listening, a body of music criticism and journalism grew. Titles like Percy Scholes's *The Listener's Guide to Music* (1919) and *The Listener's History of Music* (1923–9) signify not merely the construction of 'the listener' as an early twentieth-century project, but also the way in which listening to music – by which Percy Scholes meant the music of the European classical tradition – became a site for self-improvement. But this self-improvement was also an opportunity for consumption. All these apparent oddities – recordings of music which was not meant to be listened to without an accompanying visual drama – were desirable commodities. From the first appearance of those record-playing machines, in Western Europe and the USA at least, the listener might be an informed *critic*, or an enthusiastic *fan*, of the efforts of others, and at the same time he or she was a *consumer category*. In order to listen, the listener had to be a consumer, purchasing hardware to receive radio broadcasts and to play software media such as vinyl discs, compact cassettes or compact discs (CD) containing sonic information.

In order to service these new technologies and experiences, music was made into an object for sale. It was, in other words, 'commodified' or made into commodities, and this often involved structural alterations to the music itself; for example many pieces of classical music, jazz and pop were played slower or faster, or simply cut, to fit the sides of records (some jazz musicians still refer to a single piece of music as a 'side'; most rock musicians still refer to a single piece of music as a 'track', whether it is for a CD album or for live performance). In much of the world 'the listener' was also therefore 'the consumer'. A significant shift in the balance between these two categories took place throughout the century, though at different speeds depending on local economic and political conditions. In the USA, for example, music was always a commodity category, though structured within notions of high and low art; but in the Communist countries of China and Soviet Russia (and in Eastern Europe under Soviet influence, from 1945–89), the listener was a different category from his or her Western counterpart. Whether classical or folk, music intended to reinforce national pride was produced by national musical corporations, and although there were local recording industries with record labels such as the Russian Melodiya, the Romanian Electrecord and the Hungarian Hungaroton, music was hardly commodified at all before the early 1990s.

In Western Europe the shift towards pure commodification accelerated in the final quarter of the twentieth century as the level of subsidy for classical music fell, and broadcasters and record companies therefore started to sell it more aggressively. One important symbol of this shift is the fate of two British publications which had contributed to the formation of 'the listener' as both critical project and consumer category. *The Listener*, a BBC magazine dedicated to critical listening strategies and responses to broadcast sound, was first published in 1929 as a companion to the corporation's more straightforward listings magazine *The Radio Times*. *The Listener* was closed in 1976, a generation after its parent company had started to make images as well as sounds for broadcast. *The Gramophone*, meanwhile, has remained an important magazine (and latterly website) since its foundation in 1923, its reviews helping the classical enthusiast in particular to explore both the mainstream and the byways of commercial recorded music.

This critical listener and consumer was imagined, and implicitly addressed, as male. The technologies of recording and broadcasting gradually transfigured the home, providing an alternative to the domestic piano. Since more women than men played piano, this change therefore displaced one aspect of skilled domestic femininity. Indeed, when broadcasters imagined their female audiences, even the skill of listening was denied them. The head of the BBC local station Radio Essex gave the following invocation in 1985: 'We call our average listener Doreen. She lives in Basildon. She isn't stupid but she's only listening with half an ear, and doesn't necessarily understand long words'.[4] These patronising gendered assumptions were hardly new. One of the standard columns in the 1950s *Listener* was 'broadcast suggestions for the housewife'; these recipes and hints for looking after cut flowers were worlds away from the serious cultural and political criticism offered in the rest of the magazine.

With the BBC's deliberately highbrow programming, the Third Programme (relaunched in 1967 as Radio Three), the assumption was reversed: material was provided for an educated male who was imagined to be in control of the domestic listening equipment, and to be using it to listen intently with both ears. Modes of music diffusion governed by listener choice, such as radio tuners, record turntables and cartridges, tape and CD players and their associated amplifiers and loudspeakers, notably the more upmarket forms of these devices known collectively as hi-fi, are among the few domestic technologies associated with masculinity, as are collections of recordings. It was accepted that listening to the sounds of the contemporary world was an important personal and social attribute. In the nineteenth century city Jean Baudelaire imagined the 'flâneur', the male observer, who enjoyed the shape of modern urban life by wandering the streets and observing. The twentieth-century equivalent, also implicitly male, was content to retire to a small room, close the curtains from the visible world, and listen, through equipment he had 'domesticated', made part of the private space of the household.

The concept of 'domestication' means more than simply 'of the home'; it also implies a certain amount of familiarity and ease of use. This idea of 'domestication' was developed in the 1950s by sociologists who wanted to describe and account for the ways in which new technologies became integrated into the daily routines of the household. This means that in a symbolic sense, domesticated technologies can be seen to be a necessary part of the family, almost as 'friends' – communication devices like the radio, television and telephone all became 'domesticated' in this sense during the twentieth century. However, this process of domestication carries with it particular dangers for the household, as the arrival of new technologies performing similar functions are *not* symbolic friends in the same way as existing objects, and they can threaten or disrupt the environment before they are domesticated in their turn.

4   Stephen Barnard, *On the Radio*, Milton Keynes 1989, p.43

The domestication of music technologies started at the end of the nineteenth century. The gramophone's first popularity coincided with the introduction of the telephone, though this was in most parts of the world a more public device, in two ways: firstly through the 'phone boxes' installed on public streets when domestic phone lines were not universal. Secondly and more subtly, where telephones were installed they would often be in the 'hallway' of the middle-class house (more easily accessible by servants and house-guests), rather than the family space of the living room or the individualised privacy of the bedroom. The gramophone, on the other hand, was usually in the household's principal living space, and it was therefore often made as well-crafted furniture rather then a utilitarian object – encasing them in familiar-looking wooden structures such as Chippendale-style cabinets was one way in which these strange new devices were 'domesticated'. Similarly, after the first flush of technology-enthusiasts' devices which emphasised their newness through stark, functional metal-cased designs, the radio, as a potential object for family listening round the hearth, was also usually built into a stylish wooden cabinet. From the 1950s the same points could be made about television, and most forms of domestic music technology sold at that time, the 'radiogram' or the 'stereogram', were crafted in traditional-looking or, in the 1960s, modernist Scandinavian pine cabinets: the results looked like an amalgam of the sea chest and the coffee table, though with openings or slatted grilles for loudspeakers.

Most advertisements for domestic hi-fi equipment are, and were, explicitly gendered. In the year 1955, for example, we find several advertising campaigns for hi-fi products in the pages of *The Listener* and *The Gramophone*. The small number of ads which featured illustrations of women – such as a series of adverts for RDG radiograms which depict the very glamorous Lady Barnett, pictured in evening wear – all draw attention to the hi-fi unit as a piece of furniture. Most, however, illustrate men as connoisseurs and users of the equipment itself. A series of ads, carried in both magazines, for the Pye Black Box record player is worth attention. The Black Box was a semi-portable device available in various finishes, from a (cheaper) plain rectangular box, to an ornately japanned – lacquered and decorated in Japanese style – piece of furniture. All these adverts were fronted by photographic images of the Black Box itself and each also featured a cartoonish black and white drawing of an individual man. The men are of different ages and social classes, and the accompanying copy tries to imitate their vocalisation; for example a middle aged, moustachioed upper-middle-class man in formal evening wear, seen adjacent to the most expensive version of the Black Box, claims that he 'might as well be in the opera house. All due to something called Hi Fi, so they tell me'.[5] A couple of weeks later a chubby middle-aged man, sporting a less

---

5   *The Listener*, 8 February 1955, p.15

extravagant moustache and wearing a light three-piece business suit, says that the Black Box captures the sound of a brass band perfectly, and in a mock northern accent tells us that 'by gum, it fair makes t'blood tingle… it's Hi Fi lad, that's what it is'.[6]

In the same year *The Listener* carried an advert for a new Grundig tape recorder model, with a photograph of the tape recorder alongside a somewhat unprepossessing balding middle-aged man, sitting and leaning confidentially towards the viewer. He tells us that he is 53 years old, and that he used to build his own recording equipment, but he is now a convert to commercial technology. He deliberates on the advantages of buying a ready-made machine, as opposed to making his own:

> I look at my Grundig, I switch it on and I'm surrounded with music from three speakers – three-dimensional recording they call it – just like that. I have to chuckle when I think of the early days. In the pre-electric recording days we used to build enormous and complicated acoustic speakers to get the most out of the old soundbox… more recently it was pickups and thorn needles and speakers set in solid concrete and wires and more wires. The silly thing was I never got round to hearing music. Nothing was ever finished. Ask my wife. She had to dust the place.[7]

This explicitly gendered division of labour (and of listening) was echoed by P. Wilson's technical column in *The Gramophone*: enthusiastically reviewing the new stereo technologies in October 1955 he boasts that 'my wife is already resigned to having two holes in the wall in our new home!'[8]

What the new hi-fi of the 1950s offered, then, is clearly a particular mode of 'domestication', in this case the domestication of men as well as machines. These advertisements represent one aspect of a gradual shift in the representation of the middle-class man's role in the home, from the maker of the environment, as doer, builder, and master of technology, to man as the mere consumer of ready-made materials, reinforcing the home as the place of the working man's rest and recuperation, and celebrating the domestication of the technology and the music alike. Here, for instance, is the copy associated with a drawing of a young, clean-shaven man, pipe in hand, in another of that 1955 series of advertisements for the Pye Black Box (which is this time shown in its plainest, and cheapest, finish):

---

6 *The Listener*, 22 February 1955, p.22
7 *The Listener*, 17 November 1955, p.23
8 *The Gramophone*, 8 October 1955, p.126

Concertos can be costly… after all, it's not merely the cost of a good seat, but a trip to town and supper after the concert can soon knock holes in a budget – mine, at least. With the Black Box, I sit in the best seat in the house (my favourite chair). Listening with my eyes closed, the orchestra seems to fill the room. With my pipe going nicely, I want nothing more. [9]

Notions of value and discrimination are embodied through the innovations in the 'quality' of the sound inherent in the product (the three speakers in the Grundig tape recorder, the 'hi-fi' status of the Pye Black Box), and not so much in the music itself; wanting to shift units, manufacturer Pye is as happy to be seen in the brass band admirer's as in the opera lover's home.

41

In the early twenty-first century the selling of hi-fi is no longer so directly associated with the production of masculinity and connoisseurship. The Bowers & Wilkins (B&W) loudspeakers company website is among the many registers of this shift. B&W is a British company started in Sussex in 1967 by two electronic engineers who were also classical music enthusiasts. They developed their products with the intention of providing acoustically transparent renderings of live musicians' capabilities. At 1970s sales demonstrations, a live musician – say, a cellist – would perform, at some point a recording made by the same musician replayed through B&W loudspeakers would replace her, and those present were challenged to tell when the live performance had stopped and the speakers had taken over. B&W's focus on this notion of authentic 'high fidelity' – in other words, faithfulness to an original source – meant that their products were taken seriously by music producers and sound engineers alike. Many classical recordings still carry the imprimatur 'monitored using B&W speakers', and the company proudly reported early in 2006 on the refurbishment of EMI's world-famous Abbey Road studios, incorporating its latest 800 series speakers, featuring trademark (and very expensive) tweeter units manufactured from diamond.

Nonetheless the company has moved beyond the desire simply to embody the conservative hi-fi values of faithfulness to the source. As early as 1983 B&W was using the prefix 'DM', as in 'digital monitor', for its products; the adoption of woven Kevlar (the material used in body armour) for speaker cones is among its technical innovations. The product range has diversified in scope, to include home cinema, in-wall and whole-house systems, and a number of designs which are advertised as specifically 'cool' looking – as well as efficient. All these middle and upmarket products were promoted in the mid-2000s through a series of images of very sterile 'home' environments with no obvious human presence. Polished wooden floors, flawless drapes, sunlit sofas facing wall-

---

[9] *The Listener*, 23 April 1955, p.17

mounted widescreen televisions and hi-fi equipment (with no visible cables connecting the various components!) seem to offer a world in which 'domestication' exists for the benefit of the equipment, and humans are tolerated at best as the suppliers of power to the units on display. There's nothing obviously associated with the presence of children in these images: no toys, and definitely no untidiness. It's a 'domestic' environment, but hardly familial.

42   Where the B&W website did use images of people, they were significant of a particular attitude to music. A number of talking heads – all white men – discussed aspects of the design and manufacture of the more innovative and expensive products. The company website also carried, again in promotion of its upmarket 800 series range, a number of taster interviews by celebrity B&W owners such as classical pianist Alfred Brendel, rock musicians Dave Stewart (formerly of Eurythmics) and Peter Gabriel (former Genesis singer and subsequently the leading light of the WOMAD festivals), jazz singer and record producer Cassandra Wilson, and dance music composer and entrepreneur Matt Black (of Coldcut, and co-founder of the dance music label Ninja Tune). Each of them had performed and recorded music for a promotional DVD which was available from the website. It's notable that all these musical celebrities are established mid- or late-career performers, and none deal in out-and-out pop; it might be assumed that the company sells its relatively expensive products principally to those in their thirties and beyond, just as Pye and Grundig did in the 1950s.

Arcam is another relatively successful British hi-fi manufacturer, founded in 1976 by graduates of Cambridge University, with its R&D and main factory still situated in one of that city's science parks. Again, this company has boasted of technical innovation, including the use of processing circuits for CD players adapted from defence systems technologies. It has always provided for a middlebrow musical environment. Rather than demonstrating that a live 'cello will sound like a recording and vice versa, Arcam has tended to provide lists of commercial recordings which they claimed would best demonstrate the capabilities of their equipment. The music cited in their promotional material is all – like those B&W celebrity users – Anglo-American mainstream popular, jazz or light classical music, available on major record labels, performed by people in mid- or late career (examples include pop and rock by George Michael, Crowded House, REM, Sheryl Crow, and Madonna; jazz from guitarist Pat Metheny and tenor sax player Sonny Rollins; and the Academy of St Martin in the Fields, conducted by Sir Neville Marriner, playing music by Vivaldi). What seems important here is not so much the accurate transmission of nuanced *performance*, but of nuanced *sonic information* to the listener. This is a form of 'authenticity' which fetishises the disc player, the amplification equipment and loudspeakers, and the production values of the recording rather than the composition or the performance. Such an attitude owes something to the notion of hi-fi, but nothing to any sense of genre hierarchy – indeed hierarchies of musical value are produced here not by genre, but through the ability of equipment to generate an accurate transmission of what has been recorded (e.g. clear deep bass notes or unsibilant vocals). Clearly, like the B&W marketing through celebrity musicians, among the important facets of Arcam's marketing strategy is to present to the consumer an uncontroversial, easily accessible list of test recordings which show their equipment to advantage, signalling that their products – however technologically advanced – are not designed for the reproduction of any particular musical tradition, but will improve the sound of any (middlebrow) music.

The 2006 promotional brochure for the Arcam DV79 DVD audio/video player (available on its website as a PDF document at the time of writing) goes one stage further than this unchallenging musical technophilia.[10] The brochure is not designed around the usual hard-focus photograph of the unit itself – though there is one – but instead is dominated by a much more interesting image which features a carefully soft-focused black and white photograph of two men and two women. All are slim, apparently in their late twenties or early thirties, and apparently black, Asian or 'mixed-race'. The image signals the connection the manufacturers and advertisers wish to make with the vibrant new information economy of the contemporary multicultural city such as London or Paris, New York or Los Angeles, or indeed Delhi, Shanghai or Sao Paolo. The youngish people are pictured sitting on a sofa, glasses of red wine in hand, and smiling delightedly at each other. There is no obvious connection between this image and the particular piece of technology on offer; or with film or music as such; or with watching DVD video or listening to music through Arcam products, for that matter.

The contrast with those images of middle-aged white men which were used to sell Pye and Grundig products in the 1950s couldn't be clearer. What is on offer in this kind of advertising is a rather different set of possibilities of 'domestication' which no longer assumes the heterosexual nuclear family as the basic domestic unit, or that married men in their 50s are the principal spenders on and users of hi-fi equipment. Single people of either sex, gay or straight, and flat-sharers, are recognised as among the potential customers. These twenty-first century middle- and upmarket hi-fi manufacturers are therefore less obviously involved with the production of gender differences within the household than those selling hi-fi in the 1950s; they are, similarly, less interested in the marketing of a narrow kind of musical connoisseurship than in catering for a relatively broad range of musical tastes. But they are also

---

[10] www.arcam.co.uk/downloads/DV79brochure.pdf, accessed 18 September 2006

selling an image. The emphasis is now on the household as the setting for that bleakest of contemporary terms, 'lifestyle *choice*', in which the choice of design of the house or flat and its furnishings and the *display* of its technological components – whether the technologies on show are hi-fi in the living room or double fan-ovens in the kitchen – becomes a substitute for the actual *use* of those components to generate meanings for their owners, partly because those owners are working all the hours of the day in order to pay for it all and have very little time either to cook or to listen. Such advertising promotes a form of conspicuous consumption reflexive of social status but not of musical taste or knowledge. We're a long way from Grundig Man's DIY technophilia, but also from Dave Hill's musical friendship, which was based around the time-rich mutual appreciation of rock and soul records, not the time-poor display values of the equipment they were played on.

So what is the meaning of music to most of those who want to use it as part of a 'lifestyle'? Kevin Dettmar's interesting 2006 survey of attitudes to the music, *Is Rock Dead?* would seem to indicate that as music passes into lifestyle accessory, it ceases to command attention. Dettmar discusses the strange case of Nick Hornby, the author of *High Fidelity* (a 1997 novel which was filmed in 2000, directed by Stephen Frears and starring John Cusack as the narrating record-shop owner). *High Fidelity* is a witty and cleverly disguised boy-meets-girl story where the romantic happy ending is postponed almost indefinitely because of the narrator's obsessive interest in rock, soul and pop records. But by the time the film was released Hornby himself had less than obsessive ideas about the place of music in his own life, and he wrote a series of reviews of music for the *New York Times* which were scathing about anything which demanded attention and/or improved on repeated listening. There was no time for all that, opined Hornby. What he, and he assumed his readers, wanted was easy listening music with immediate impact. Everything else – including some of the more complex music he himself had liked when younger – was for teenagers. This is an odd reversal of the usual marketers' assumption that pop music is for kids, who have short attention spans, and that only adults can fully appreciate complexity in lyrics and song structure.

This semantic shift away from music as a focused object of knowledge is reflected in changes in music criticism. Listening as a skill done by and discussed by men at home, was supported in the public sphere by a particular discourse of value and discrimination which was shared by music criticism on classical music, jazz, and the equally masculinised rock criticism found in the music newspapers known as the 'inkies'. The values are comparable whether we read the classical music appreciation in *The Listener* and *The Gramophone*, or the jazz criticism from the *Melody Maker* of the 1930s–1950s, or the rock criticism which *Rolling Stone, Melody Maker, Rock File* and *New Musical Express* (NME) featured from the late-1960s onwards.

The rock journalism of the 1960s and after was characterised by writing which attempted to promote a 'rock aesthetic'. Music by young, well-educated men was privileged; the sex-drugs-rock'n'roll lifestyle was lauded, and journalists such as Nick Kent thought themselves to be at least the equal of the musicians they interviewed. In the USA the longest-lasting rock music magazine has been *Rolling Stone*, which was founded in San Francisco in 1967. *Rolling Stone* hired male journalists with a fine command of prose and a self-important sense of judgment, such as Greil Marcus, and it tried to avoid the internal culture, and the political and psychedelic excesses of the underground press – though most would agree that *Rolling Stone's* finest hour was in the 1970s, when it featured the work of the writer Hunter S. Thompson, who was closer to those political and psychedelic excesses than most people would ever want to be.

This type of criticism has been challenged from many quarters. *Smash Hits* (a colourful weekly UK paper founded in 1977, and which after a decade of sales decline was closed in February 2006) might seem to be a particular kind of exception, in that it was principally targeted at girls and young women, and it was cheerfully fascinated with the ephemeral side of pop. In fact the paper was founded and edited by the same type of well-educated middle-class men as the writers for *NME*, so it was perhaps unsurprising when Mark Ellen and David Hepworth, each of whom had been a former editor of Smash Hits, founded *Q* in 1985. Like *Rolling Stone* and the French paper *Les Inrockuptibles*, *Q* is part of the same story of middle-class men writing about and valorising the musics they like according to elitist canons of taste.

At first these two publications may seem totally different. While *Smash Hits* seemed to live in the perpetual present, only interested in whoever was involved with the hits of that moment, *Q* was principally interested in the past. From the start it was a nostalgic publication, busily trying to manufacture a 'canon' of great artists and albums, which in the early days meant that its journalists discussed what these might be, at some length, in multi-page feature articles. Its first-ever cover star was Paul McCartney. Nonetheless despite the relentlessly cheerful and irreverent nature of *Smash Hits* and the forelock-tugging critical-historical approach of *Q*, in one very important sense each publication was a variation of the other. Both were working on the mainstream music industry's behalf, dedicated to the selling of a limited range of musical products, and in *Q's* case this emphasis became starkly clear in its third decade, as the long articles on great artists and albums were reduced all too often to lists of, say, '100 great albums that you need to hear before you die', and the like – all of which albums are mainstream major-label products, and most of which are by ageing white men (though a 2006 survey for publishers EMAP found that the readership of these magazines was increasingly female, and the magazines' content began to change in response).

The change from criticism to cataloguing has not been confined to rock. *The Listener*, when discussing classical music, was discursive, even controversially critical, and assumed a high level of general education in the reader. The more recent *BBC Music* magazine has an ethos of the provision of a guide to listening for people without any training in music appreciation, or performance, or music history. The magazine evokes the approach which had been adopted by Percy Scholes in the 1920s; indeed most contemporary music magazines and websites, whether the classical magazine *BBC Music*, the Naxos record label website, or the rock magazine and website *Q* – are based around lists and introductory guides of this sort: offering information and received wisdom rather than engaged critical knowledge, they produce hierarchies of values among composers, artists, producers, recordings, record labels and so on which the uninformed reader is invited not to engage with but to accept.

To this end the 1990s witnessed a deluge of companions to popular music's history. Pop scholarship, in the very basic sense of lists of records and chart positions such as the *Guinness Book of Hit Singles*, and discographies such as the *Goldmine Standard Catalogue of Rhythm & Blues Records*, mushroomed. Useful companions for DJ, journalist, and record/CD/MP3 collector alike, they are inclusive, offering little or nothing of selection and valuation. More recent products have taken two forms which signal a greater anxiety to order knowledge. Firstly there have been a plethora of encyclopaedic guides, offering alphabetical entries covering forms and performers. Some of their function has been archaeological (e.g. there were many mid-1990s books on women musicians, which recovered work which has been hidden from history). Much of this encyclopaedic tendency, however, has to do with the construction of a canon – all these books include as well as exclude, and all allocate praise or blame to particular acts, particular albums, and so on. They select; they produce value. But in trying to do so, they face significant challenges from the new ordering of popular knowledge which has emerged in the digital age.

Throughout popular music's history journalism has been a companion to the music itself. Newspapers routinely incorporate pop criticism; lifestyle magazines vie with dedicated music magazines in the breadth of their coverage – and the internet threatens to replace them. The internet, which hosts millions of pages on music appreciation, has hastened the closure of magazines and fanzines, and at the same time it has encouraged the broadcasting and globalising of fandom. Information about any artist is available through official and fan sites, so the tour information and the feature interview which helped to sell the magazines is no longer so necessary in print form. While this has encouraged the development of a new breed of web journalist, and a new profession of online journalism (much of it poorly paid, if at all), it has also facilitated the rise of the defiantly amateur critic, and the viral spread of amateur opinion, through the fansite, the blog, personal pages such as those on MySpace, and the online review.

The online seller Amazon, for example, has a well-used facility through which users contribute unpaid reviews of material such as books, films and CDs. This for example, taken from Amazon.co.uk, reviews the Red Hot Chili Peppers' 2006 double CD *Stadium Arcadium* (punctuation and spelling are as in the original):

> Having listened to this album throughout three times, I can safetly say that you could drop 13 songs and have one of the Chili's greatest album's since blood sugar sex magic. The great songs on this album reflect the diversity that span the Chili's music over the last twenty years. However there are some tame formula tunes on here that would of made b-sides. Stand out tracks include Hump-de-bump, 21st century, snow (hey oh) c-mon girl and animal bar, which isn't that many out of 28! so do yourself a favour and make your own 'club arcadium' complilation on your ipod.[11]

This semi-literate posting on a widely read site is, apparently, an example of the democratisation of the taste-forming process, finally confirming the tendency of the 'underground' press of the 1960s and the punk fanzines of the 1970s and removing it from the over-educated elite which has tended to hold down jobs on magazines such as *Rolling Stone*, and therefore lead opinion. Many publishers and artists are unhappy about the way in which the increasing democracy of opinion has increased the flow of abusively negative criticism, and Amazon and similar sites have occasionally been threatened with legal action by unhappy publishers, authors and musicians who find it inconvenient to read what people actually think of their books and CDs.

Professional criticism was at risk from another quarter well before these types of e-criticism became popular. The amateur review and the online-community encyclopaedia must be seen in the context of a wider shift in the mechanisms of public valuation: its move towards the culture of prizes and awards rather than review by an establishment of cultural leaders and journalists. The world of awards is the centre of what has been called the new 'economy of prestige' in relation to capitalist cultural production, which now characterises the entertainment business as a whole. The *Victoires de la Musique* awards in France and the BRIT Awards in the UK are among many examples of public award ceremonies for music based loosely on the American Film Academy's prize ceremony, the Oscars. These ceremonies are usually broadcast on primetime television; they are organised in part by the music business, and generally speaking they serve its interests by allocating awards to artists and albums which are already very successful. It's noteworthy that since the music

---

[11] The reviewer is identified as Mr Neil Kelly idlechat666, London. The website was accessed 27 November 2006.

business has tried to commodify classical music in order to sell it in the same manner as pop it has needed similar award schemes, and sure enough both the Victoires and the BRITS have launched separate awards for classical music. It's also worth noting that in each case there are also separate ceremonies for the classical awards; the commodification of 'classical music' as a category depends on its preserving some notional difference from pop and rock, even though the marketing strategies for these differentiated commodities may be exactly the same.

This is a significant shift. For most of the twentieth century, broadcasting played an important part in the creation and maintenance of the generic boundaries which informed the notion of the critical listener; the original critical-listening object was European classical music. Radio was the lynchpin which ensured that classical music topped the generic hierarchies. While the commercial stations in the USA, and monopolist European stations such as the BBC, adopted different strategies, each tended to solidify 'classical music' as an elite consumer category. In the USA, broadcasts of mainstream repertoire by star conductors with European backgrounds, such as Arturo Toscanini and Leopold Stokowski, helped to create a conservative listening public, with Toscanini constructed as a broadcasting and recording artist thanks to his work with the NBC Symphony Orchestra (a band which was put together solely for radio broadcasts) while Stokowski's fame came in part from his conducting of Disney's edutainment cartoon *Fantasia*. The BBC insisted from its foundation in 1926 onwards that the corporation's cultural mission was to educate as well as to entertain. This led to its subsidy of classical music, including the commissioning of new music, which began in the late1920s and peaked from the mid-1960s to the mid-1970s, though it survived into the new century in modified form. In *The Listener* in the 1950s, the word 'music' meant only music from this tradition, despite the fact that the BBC, in fulfilment of the 'entertainment' part of its brief, gave significant airtime to other forms of music. (*The Gramophone*, on the other hand, as a servant of the music business as a whole, was broader in coverage but very strictly hierarchical; recorded classical music featured on the front cover and the first two-thirds of the magazine, and technical discussions about hi-fi, and reviews of jazz, light music, and the emerging category of 'pop' all had to make do with the rest, including the back page advertising space.)

From the 1920s onwards, then, the place of classical music was guaranteed by broadcasting – and thanks to the reach of imperial and trading relations, it was guaranteed worldwide. The association of western art music and new technology helped to underline the enthusiasm for its continuance by the founders of Sony, who built their first machines in the rubble of post-war Tokyo. Sony co-founder Akio Morita had long been a devotee of records featuring music by Bach and Mozart, and also of his family's Victrola gramophone which played them; so he started to manufacture record and tape players of his own. Morita went on to build a globally successful company whose innovations (including in 1957 the world's first pocket-sized portable radio, and in 1979 the Walkman) transformed the relationships between sound, 'public' and 'private' space. The Walkman was the first Sony device which was deliberately marketed as a tool for the diffusion of popular music. Otherwise, the cumulative development of successive recording formats in the second half of the century – including the long-playing (LP) vinyl disc, the audio compact cassette and the audio compact disc (CD) – replicated the value structure within radio broadcasting, confirming the hegemony of the Austro-German symphonic tradition by enabling the listener to hear longer stretches of music without interruption, and so enabling domestic record consumption to mimic the uninterrupted radio broadcast as much as the ritual concentration of the concert hall. The hegemony of the concert tradition of Western classical music, as reinforced by broadcasting and the LP record, even helped to determine the format of audio software products. The CD, the first consumer format to use digital encoding, was co-developed by Philips and Sony in the late 1970s and launched in 1981. The time available for music reproduction on the standard size 12 cm CD was set at a maximum of 74 minutes in length, at the insistence of the then chairman of Sony, Norio Ohga (who was an experienced conductor of Western classical music). This seemingly very arbitrary limit – why not 75, or 60 or 90 minutes, as on an audio cassette? – was chosen in order to accommodate a single complete performance of Beethoven's Ninth Symphony on a CD, without the listener having to change discs. The world's first digital domestic music format was engineered to serve classical music.

49

Music in public space

Despite the increasing importance of the domestic and personal spheres as the site of musical reception throughout the twentieth century, public space also remained important in the commercial diffusion of music. During the twentieth century new types of venue from small jazz and folk clubs catering for a few hundred people at most, to sports stadia seating tens of thousands for globally successful rock bands, became important additions to the existing venues for dance, music hall or vaudeville entertainment, and concert music, each of which relies on a sense of people-in-public as active and informed listeners or participant consumers.

But from the 1950s onwards the music business also provided music which is avowedly not for active participation, nor for 'the listener', but designed to be only semi-audible even when loud. But the motivation for this provision of music as an aural safety blanket was research which showed that the behaviour of consumers could be modified – into moving faster on railway concourses, or spending more in shops – through the provision of the right music. So, through technologies such as the juke box, in-store radio, in-pub MTV, the hotel-lift and shopping-mall muzak (a term which indicates music provided by the Muzak Corporation), the 'general public' were in a sense drugged by sound into certain predictable forms of behaviour – modes of purchasing and consumption which were associated, through the music, with an easily transferable sense of lifestyle and life-cycle. Thanks to these public diffusion technologies, commercial popular music became pervasive in this semi-audible form during the later twentieth century. It was hard to find urban public spaces anywhere in the world without it.

However, the category of 'semi-audible music' had already emerged earlier in the century to accompany a rather different kind of collective experience – film. Coming into being at around the same time as sound recording, but developing separately as a technology until the 1920s, film helped to transfigure the awareness of sound in public space when the development of 'talkies' (films with soundtracks, from the late 1920s) led to increasing opportunities for composers. They responded by transposing aspects of folk, popular and classical musical traditions into their scores, in a way which was foreign to the concert hall. Film in India, for instance, quickly developed a hybrid soundtrack style whose composers and performers had to be equally adept in Western and Eastern performance styles. Comparatively few people noticed these tendencies or made much of them: film music was judged as more or less appropriate to the films' dramatic and emotional structures, and seldom studied in its own right. Music for film was indeed semi-audible: it was experienced, rather than actively listened to.

When listening *was* encouraged, however, the changing presentation of music in public spaces contributed to the changing of genre boundaries and collective musical taste. The spaces devoted to certain types of music had economic, political and cultural consequences. Three examples. At the Cotton Club in late 1920s Harlem the Duke Ellington Orchestra, a black band playing at a whites-only club in this mainly black residential area of New York, helped to create 'jazz' as an exotic consumer category which was then sold onwards – as recordings – to what was at that point an increasingly Americaphile Europe. In the 1960s the Vienna Opera House was among the most important symbolic repositories for the culture of an international, and increasingly wealthy, middle-class, which spent much of its time conspicuously consuming expensive cultural products such as opera. This relationship helped the Decca label to record much of the standard operatic repertoire for sale, largely using the Vienna Philharmonic Orchestra and Viennese recording facilities. Again, in the same decade, following the example of established events such as the Newport Jazz Festival, outdoor rock festivals such as the first Woodstock, in 1968, or the free concert in London's Hyde Park by the Rolling Stones in the summer of 1969, helped to create 'rock' as a category almost independent from pop, in which sales were based on albums rather than the less profitable but promotionally important singles, and thereafter some bands (such as Pink Floyd) went for years without releasing any singles, but made a fortune nonetheless.

These festivals helped to establish a festival circuit which remains an important part of rock culture. Festivals have added rock and pop to cultural tourism as wealth increases among baby-boomers and their children and grandchildren. As well as the better-known events, there is a European culture circuit of alternative rock festivals. Ilosaari Rock, a three-day festival held in a sports stadium on the outskirts of the town of Joensuu, in the Karelia area in the east of Finland, celebrated its thirty-fifth year in 2006. Since 1998, Ilosaari Rock has been part of an organisation called, I'm afraid, 'Yourope', a circuit of European summer outdoor rock festivals run in sixteen countries, all with camping and family-friendly facilities, most with a wide range of performance genres on show, and almost all of which make a point of showcasing national-local acts alongside a general shared policy of 'promoting the cross-border exchange of live music talent'. Ilosaari Rock, for example, will always have more Scandinavian metal than the European average – though the headline acts of each festival are in most cases Anglo-American. This is, in other words, the musical world of the various MTV European services put on in a field, and attended by an increasingly polyglot audience of camper-van rock fans ranging in age from early teens to late fifties.

Twenty years after the shift to rock, a new type of outdoor festivity, 'acid house parties' or 'raves' (which were imported into northern Europe from Spanish holiday islands such as Ibiza) also helped to produce a new quasi-independent popular musical form. These somewhat spontaneous, anarchic and usually illegal outdoor events (and equally illegal indoor parties in abandoned warehouses, which were also widespread in the late 1980s) became more formalised under the pressures of police activity, press-driven moral panics and hostile legislation, and by the end of the 1980s licensed dance music clubs catering for large numbers of people had appeared. Compilation CD albums were issued under the titles of these clubs – such as Renaissance, Cream and the Ministry of Sound – in which the listener was addressed through the production of sequences of tracks, synchronised and mixed by DJs as if they were performing live. So these albums functioned domestically as a memory of, and a substitute for, the experience of 'raving', bringing the pleasures of the event back to the consumer's mind. Live albums made from rock concerts and festivals, classical orchestras' live CDs (which are sometimes included as part of the price of the entrance ticket), and even podcasts of radio broadcasts have a similar function as souvenirs of particular moments in space and time.

Changing the boundaries

The boundaries between public and private space are constantly being renegotiated, in part through the changing provision of music. Public space which is permeated by the semi-audible sounds of 'muzak' denies the normal mode of being of 'the listener', who must first choose the listened object, and then pay full attention. It is perhaps unsurprising, then, that alongside the flourishing of muzak, developers of the technologies which diffuse music provided a series of increasingly effective portable musical sources to enable 'the listener' to function, and to preserve his or her listening autonomy, even in the most crowded, impersonal public spaces. Small portable reel-to-reel tape recorders appeared in the 1950s, and transistor technology enabled the construction of the first pocket-sized radios in the late 1950s. At the end of the 1970s the compact cassette Walkman, and in the 1980s and 1990s similar portable CD and minidisc players, provided small, relatively cheap, portable, and – thanks to their use of headphones rather than loudspeakers – intensely personal sonic environments. Adorned by a Walkman the listener could listen to one world while observing another – for example one could listen to the sounds of a rapper from South Central Los Angeles while relaxing on a sunny beach in Goa. Through such experiences the listener's choice, in other words his or her identity as a listener, could be reinforced in most circumstances, and the manufacturers of playback equipment and magnetic media had increased personal choice while also facilitating the withdrawal of people who were physically 'in public' into their own, private, listening worlds.

In a sense this personalising of the aural environment had started in the 1930s, as car manufacturers began to fit aerials and in-dash fitting slots for car radios, and as car radios themselves became more efficient. The first Motorola car radio was sold in the USA in 1930; Blaupunkt, the leading European car radio brand, was founded in 1933. Car radios and the subsequent in-car tape and CD players make the automobile a liminal space – in other words, somewhere on the boundary between public and private – offering the traveller the chance firstly to experience a different sonic and visual environment, then to choose more and more of its parameters.

While most manufacturers now routinely incorporate stereo equipment into their vehicles, there has also been a significant development of so-called 'after-market' products offering high power and high-fidelity reproduction, which the listener-driver can choose (alongside products such as engine and exhaust upgrades, luxuriously trimmed sports seats, and flamboyant lighting and colour schemes) as part of the personalisation of these otherwise mass-market machines. After-market in-car sound systems have a semi-underground culture which celebrates them, including DVDs, websites and magazines, which are part of the wider consumer-subculture of after-market car personalisation.

Much of this culture in Japan, the USA and UK alike is organised around Japanese high-performance cars; it is commonly thought that this type of spending on the personalisation of a car is a form of 'domestication'. The car is a substitute for the houses which are simply too expensive for the average young Japanese, who remain in the parental home; so the car becomes a parallel domestic space for young people who otherwise share usually very cramped accommodation with parents and siblings. There are similar tendencies in the UK. Nonetheless, though homes are too expensive for young men and women alike, the principal spenders on modified cars are men. Gender and power are always at issue in the ways in which technologies are developed, bought and sold, and used as the expression of their owner's personality, and after-market car modification is no exception. The television format *Pimp My Ride* is an example of the public expression of this type of car modification, and since the show was first developed for MTV, it is worth remarking that this subculture is an aspect of the 'laddish' masculinity of MTV culture. In 2006, the strap line for the website www.Maxpower.co.uk, for example, announced both the site itself and *Max Power*, the magazine it promotes, in terms which make it very clear that its imagined reader is a young heterosexual male. The website claimed to be 'your portal into living the world of car modifying, super cars, the babes and the lifestyle.'

Making public space reverberate with personal music, car stereos micro-broadcast the driver's taste; the many and various (and usually very powerful) after-market amplifiers and equalisers, speakers and sub-woofers personalise a lot more than the owner's car. Perhaps the key ingredient in the package is the sub-woofer, which can make the entire car resonate with low-frequency energy as if it was a club PA system. In order to show this power to advantage, several enthusiasts make recordings with as much deep bass as possible. Here for example, the website maxpower.co.uk announces a new CD, tailor-made for the car with expensive audio, marketed by the UK's leading dance-music brand, Ministry of Sound:

> Ministry of Sound has again teamed up with audio terrorists Fuel to bring you *Maximum Bass 2*. This is a storming bass heavy monster, designed to be played extra loud. Its predecessor out sold all other bass albums in the UK and this next offering goes a step further than before, giving you the loudest, deepest, sub-blowing bass-lines ever written.[12]

The successful movie *The Fast and the Furious* (directed by Rob Cohen, 2001), its sequels *2 Fast 2 Furious* (directed by John Singleton, 2003) and *The Fast and the Furious: Tokyo Drift* (directed by Justin Lin, 2006) and the many 'underground' camcorder-based car-racing DVDs such as *2 Fast 2 Real for Hollywood*, all use contemporary popular music, mixed prominently into the films' soundtrack, as a metaphor for the power and individuality of the cars and

---

[12] www.Maxpower.co.uk, accessed 16 November 2006

their owners; each of the Hollywood movies was accompanied by a compilation soundtrack album.

This emphasis on the car as a personalised, and highly audible, sound carrier has not gone unnoticed by the major car manufacturers. Both Volvo and Volkswagen, for example, have offered optional custom speaker systems designed by Danish hi-fi manufacturer Dynaudio. The system developed by Dynaudio for the 2005 model Volkswagen Passat uses ten speakers, with the doorspaces used to increase the resonance of the woofers. Such ingenuity is common: since space is at a premium in most cars, large speakers are very difficult to fit, and the sound engineer has to encounter a bewildering variety of differently angled soft and hard surfaces. Many manufacturers are therefore indebted to the approach taken by Amar Gopal Bose, a former MIT researcher whose company, founded in 1964, developed domestic hi-fi systems which use a number of small speakers facing in different directions, rather than one or two large units facing the listener directly. Bose Corporation, like Dynaudio, has worked with a number of car manufacturers. The use of tailor-made Bose sound systems by Audi, for example, is a marketing tool which helps to sell not only cars such as the iconic TT, but also their more mundane offerings like the A3. Similarly, an Alfa Romeo model, the 159, which was launched in the UK in 2006, was advertised with the following among the technical details of performance and safety systems:

> The standard audio system, complete with CD player and parametric sound equalizer, is designed to match the specific characteristics of the passenger cabin. The [optional] Bose Hi-Fi system was also designed for Alfa Romeo. This system gives the very best sound performance and gives auditorium-quality sound reproduction, throughout the passenger cabin.[13]

That optional Bose system includes a subwoofer; so even without 'pimping' the car with obvious sonic signs of personalisation such as remapped engine control and wide-bore exhaust system, and without going to the trouble of installing an 'after-market' sound system, the proud owner of a new Alfa Romeo 159 can imprint her or his aural signature on the streets.

Music, public space and the concert: making sounds fit the space

The concert tradition began in the eighteenth century as entrepreneurs began to put on musical events for a paying public – which is essentially what happens today. Before this point opera and most of what we now think of as 'classical music' were in a sense domestic: paid for by bishops, monarchs, aristocrats and

---

[13] www.alfaromeo.co.uk, accessed 8 December 2006

other very rich people, for performance in their homes; the only other significant employers of musicians were the Church and city councils. The composer Johann Sebastian Bach (1685–1750) spent his active life first as the court musician for various aristocrats and princes, then as organist and choirmaster of the church in Leipzig. A generation later the composer Josef Haydn (1732–1809) spent most of his career as a paid employee of the Esterházy family in Hungary; he was a family servant, working mainly at their palatial country residence, and providing operas and symphonies for the family's public entertainments, or settings of the mass for their worship, or smaller-scale works such as piano sonatas or string quartets for their private time, as they wished. A relatively small amount of this work was published in Haydn's lifetime.

Most people could not afford an orchestra and choir of their own, but in the bigger European cities a few people began to realise that the middle class public *could* pay for performances collectively, by subscription. Towards the end of the eighteenth century, the practice of subscription concerts began: the entrepreneur J.P. Salomon brought Josef Haydn to London for two successful series of concerts – Haydn wrote his last twelve symphonies, still known as the 'London' symphonies, for these events. By the end of his life Haydn was a Vienna-based composer, and apparently working freelance, though he was still nominally in the service of his Hungarian patrons. Moving on another generation, but still in Vienna, Haydn's pupil Ludwig van Beethoven (1770–1827) escaped from full-time employment for one patron far earlier in his career. Most of his work thereafter was individually commissioned, and he was arguably the first composer to become a public figure: over 10,000 Viennese citizens are said to have attended his funeral.

Larger audiences meant the need for more volume. Therefore, from Beethoven onwards composers wrote for ever bigger orchestras, with larger numbers of strings, and louder brass and wind instruments, which were – increasingly – designed by engineers, and built in factories rather than individually made by craftsmen. At the beginning of the nineteenth century the average orchestra might consist of forty players; at the end of the century it was closer to a hundred. The new concert circuit made similar demands on the individual performer; so manufacturers made louder pianos, with steel frames and more powerful hammer actions – though this was in part due to the increasing physical demands of the performers on the professional concert circuit, who from Franz Liszt onwards needed an instrument which was more physically rigid and less likely to go out of tune when played hard for long periods.

Something very similar happened with jazz and dance music, and then rock music, in the twentieth century. The early-century jazz ensembles might number half a dozen people, with two or three rhythm instruments (drums, guitar or banjo, piano), bass (often a relatively loud brass instrument such as a tuba or sousaphone) and three solo instruments such as cornet or trumpet, clarinet or saxophone, and trombone. Trumpeter Louis Armstrong, arguably the first global jazz star, played in such ensembles. As the music grew in popularity, and musicians played in larger venues, the typical ensemble increased in size until the mid-1930s era of the 'big bands' led by people such as Count Basie, Duke Ellington, Woody Herman and Glenn Miller. These bands would often consist of a rhythm section of piano and drums, but now with a string bass, and a brass and reeds line-up including four trumpets, four trombones, and five reed players who would play saxophones, clarinets and/or flutes according to the composer's or arranger's wishes.

By this time there was more to an increase in volume than merely employing more players. That lone big-band string bass would have been completely lost without amplification, as would the big band's vocalist. The microphone had been invented in the 1870s, but early carbon models were inefficient and low in sound quality. The electronic microphones – with far higher-quality output – which appeared in the 1920s, and the matching development of moving coil loudspeakers, made the 'big band' possible by allowing the use of public address (PA) amplification systems which could balance the string bass, and the voice, against the power of drums, brass and reeds. As a result more people could listen and/or dance, in bigger venues.

The 1930s–40s era of the big band also saw the development of the first new electronic instruments, such as the Hammond organ which was first sold (as an instrument for churches) in 1935, and the solid-body electric guitar which was developed by Les Paul and Leo Fender in the 1940s and 1950s; in 1951 Fender also introduced the electric bass guitar, which was arguably as vital in the evolution of pop, soul and rock music as the electric guitar itself. These instruments, using amplifiers and speaker systems, could fill the dance venues of the new urban environment without the need for the dozen or so – expensively salaried – brass and reed players who were needed by the big band, and so this technical innovation meant that significant employment opportunities for musicians began to wane. As electronic instruments and their amplifiers became cheaper and more reliable, the big bands began to disappear, and meanwhile the new music of urban black Americans, rhythm'n'blues or r'n'b, became the first popular music genre to be associated, from the start, with the sound of electronic instruments.

Rock'n'roll followed r'n'b, and as this in turn mutated into the new pop of the early 1960s, the same process took place once again: larger venues meant the need for louder music. The result was the development of 'stadium rock': in this case the music becomes louder entirely through the use of technology rather than through the employment of greater numbers of musicians. In the early

1960s, pop group amplification was in its infancy. The object of guitar and bass amplifiers and PA systems was to match the level of the drums; the standard Vox combination amplifier and speaker for an electric guitar had a power output of a mere 30 watts. Groups played in relatively small environments – jazz clubs, music halls and the like – with a maximum audience of 2,000 at most. When the Beatles played at Shea Stadium on 15 August 1965, they inaugurated the era of stadium rock. Over 55,000 people crowded into this New York baseball arena to witness performances by five bands before the headline act, the Beatles themselves, played (for only half an hour). Aware of the size of the scheduled venues, Vox had made a number of new amplifiers specially for this tour, increasing the power output significantly from 30 to 100 watts, and the output from these was mixed through a PA system, but even so most of the Beatles' Shea Stadium performance was inaudible to the audience (chiefly because so many of them were screaming. The resulting television version of the concert, first broadcast in 1966, was heavily doctored in the studio, with most of the songs re-recorded by the band in sync with the existing visuals).

As a result of the Beatles' experience (and noting that stadium tours could be extremely profitable) electronics manufacturers began to build amplifiers and speaker cabinets which were more powerful and more rugged, and which could be racked in sequence to increase output. Jim Marshall, for example, started making and selling amplifiers and speaker cabinets from his London drums shop in 1962. By 1968, thanks to the ambassadorial use of the 'Marshall stack' by artists such as The Who, Cream, Deep Purple and Jimi Hendrix, demand for Marshall Amplifiers and speakers had led to the opening of a dedicated factory, with hundreds of employees.

Stadium rock was new in power, but offered the same kind of listening as the classical concert; the band played from a stage to a contained and relatively passive audience. Nonetheless new kinds of interactive fandom were developed, in which the concert public shared their experiences among themselves and with the bands they followed. This often involved bootlegging – the illegal recording of live performances, which were shared among fans. Some bands, including Metallica, and perhaps most notably the Grateful Dead, actually encouraged this aspect of their fans' cultures, since it seemed to have no impact on concert ticket or album sales. In some ways bootlegging has provided the music historian as well as the fan with an important service, archiving the histories of various performers. For example, jazz alto saxophonist Charlie Parker's fans, illegally taping his late 1940s to early 1950s concerts, provide the mass of our evidence about his evolution as a player, partly because he made fewer official recordings than we might have expected, due to industrial disputes within the American music industry, and partly because of Parker's loss through long-term heroin use of his New York cabaret card.

This private evidence of public performance through the bootleg recording, which is only encouraged by a very few artists, might be compared with the cameraphone amateur journalism which was encouraged by news gatherers in the mid-2000s, or with blogging, playlisting and other aspects of the democracy of digital culture in the new century. There are already some encouraging stories about music organisations' encouragement of new relationships with the public, such as the MIA website which has a space for fan mixes of MIA's songs; or the instant CDs of concerts given to the London Symphony Orchestra's audience as they leave the auditorium; or the podcasts of performances made available on orchestras' websites, instantly reaching larger numbers than the concert but without all the expenses of broadcasting. But many bootlegs remain illegal, sold under the counter at various informal markets or through the internet, against the wishes of the artists involved and their record labels. And we should remember that for all their long-term support of their fans' tape-swapping, it was Metallica (disgusted when an unfinished mix of a new song was broadcast on the internet) who agreed to take the lead in the American recording industry's campaign against Napster.

Personal music in public spaces

It is almost impossible these days to navigate public urban space without encountering music. Malls, town squares and the like offer a surfeit of semi-audible music, from the piped formulas of Muzak to live performances. The juke-box has all but disappeared from public houses, but it has been replaced by piped music and/or video. But during the second half of the twentieth century these manifestations of public music were challenged by people who surrounded themselves with music they had chosen: from the transistor radio to the MP3 player, this is the era of personal music in public space. It has also become the era of private–public communication. The mobile phone, an executive toy in the late 1980s, became ubiquitous in many parts of the world by the late 1990s; in doing so to an extent it *displaced* personal music players such as the Walkman. Though personal stereo then made a comeback through the MP3 player, the mobile phone may soon *replace* them in turn.

Despite the increasing encroachment of audio-visual forms as the predominant mode of entertainment, the early twenty-first century saw a revival in the use of personal stereo, through portable MP3 players. As such it helped to produce a bundle of problems concerning the role of music in an age dominated by ease of communication. MP3 is an encoding format which allows files containing music or video to be compressed, so that they can be stored without excessive use of memory. Portable devices which can store these or similar files usually function in relation to a computer which can both store copies of personal CD collections and download music from the internet. But the stand-alone MP3 player is only one among many early twenty-first century portable communications and entertainment devices including DVD players, games machines, laptops, Personal Digital Assistants (PDAs) and mobile phones, most of which have more than one function – even many iPods can store address books and calendar information. Such portable devices are therefore both a conduit for and a repository of culture – both the manufactured, ready-made cultures of the information age and the 'made' cultures which appropriate such products for their own ends, such as personalised car stereos and social networking on the internet.

In the mid-2000s, the advent of the third-generation (3G) mobile phone in effect meant the rolling up of much existing computer function into the mobile device, which was no longer 'simply' a telephone with a capacity to send brief text messages or low-resolution pictures. 3G and subsequent generation mobile communications devices can function as a PDA, or a personal entertainment centre, or both. Such machines therefore draw together two types of human memory, making the device a type of prosthetic addition to the user's brain. Firstly, they can contain all the functions of the diary and contact list – which are aspects of the *personal* memory that have often, historically, been stored in devices like the diary, telephone book or Filofax. Secondly, they can contain, or give access to, the *collective* memory of the culture as a whole, which has expanded the encyclopaedias and monographs, archives and museums of print and material culture – and their catalogues and databases – and is largely available via the internet. Such information was only available before the 1990s piecemeal, in the world's great libraries, archives, museums and art galleries; it is now available online. Music is only one aspect of this massive cultural availability.

The 3G (and later) mobile device can mediate all these functions through the virtual communities of email chat and phone text message groups, fan and personal websites, blogs and so on. It has the potential, therefore, to implement such subjects' engagement with culture as a whole. For many users, both because of the facilitation of communication and access to information, and the ease with which it can be personalised, the mobile phone is vital in the construction and performance of identity.

As with the attention-seeking music system in the personalised car, arguably the most important badge of personalisation associated with mobile telephony is music. At first this was only usual through one of the most attenuated forms of music, the ringtone. It was announced in the *Guardian* newspaper in August 2003 that downloaded ringtones, most of them very brief melodies taken from current pop which retailed in the UK at £3.50 each, were outselling the pop singles from which they were derived, which retailed for less than £2.[14] Music-as-ringtone is a way in which to personalise an industrial product, helping to

---

[14] 'Ringing the Changes – Music moguls must join the Revolution', leading article, www.guardian.co.uk, accessed 13 August 2003

make it a prosthetic aspect of the user's identity as well as just memory. A 30-second personal identity signal makes publicly audible what the Walkman or iPod confer in relative silence: where the personal stereo maintains the private in public space, we must note that the mobile phone's ringtone can – just like in-car hi-fi – far more aggressively privatise public space in order for the user to navigate it on his or her own terms rather than those of the shopkeepers, local councils etc. who provide the semi-audible musical background noise of everyday life. The mobile, rather than the MP3 player, is in this sense potentially the consummate contemporary cultural object, as the ringtone, the musical sign of its carrier's identity, takes forward the historical dialogue between technology and culture, public and private space. Mobile phones, ringtones and personal music signify that *public space is (now) virtual domestic space*.

However, the increasing potential of the internet-connected 'phone' to access almost all knowledge, from almost anywhere in the world, also makes it part of the most significant problem facing the entertainment industry. Much of the knowledge which is stored on the internet is freely accessible, including copyrighted entertainment material, which is to many users part of the 'free' knowledge base. However, to the owners or originators of copyright material, free access to this material is theft. Most of the early retailers of ringtones, for example, were small businesses which paid scant regard to the legal rights of the owners of copyrights in the fragmentary tunes they were selling.

The phenomenon of the ringtone was at this point, therefore, just another manifestation of the long struggle between the makers of recorded music (including composers, artists, record companies and publishers) and the manufacturers of recording technologies, which has been going on since the middle of the twentieth century. In this struggle the former has consistently campaigned against all the latter's technological innovations, such as audio cassette, digital audio tape or DAT, recordable CD, or MP3 players. Since 2001 the worldwide recording industry, backed in most cases by national governments, has taken action against the owners and software writers of P2P programmes such as Napster and Kazaa, which allow users to disseminate digitally encoded music files by accessing and copying from each others' collections. Subsequent to the first wave of cases against software developers and websites, the Recording Industry Association of America and the British Phonograph Industry, among other national bodies acting for record labels, have also taken legal action against individual users of swapped files. Among the carriers of such files are 3G mobile phones, many of which can access the internet directly, can exchange files between phones and/or computers using Bluetooth, and can store MP3 files, whether or not they were obtained legally.

Private sound, privatised public space

Thinking about portable communications/entertainment devices in this way leads to consideration of the wider interactions within and among culture, community, communication and consumption. Exploring these questions will expand our means of conceptualising notions of identity, self, mind and body in what may constitute a new paradigm in both market and cultural relating, and in social and/or cultural policy. We – and that's all of us who use these technologies, not just a few marketing experts or sociologists – need to reflect on the ways in which the interplay of capital and culture, technology and identity are and will be expressed through the uses of music, as portable devices become more powerful, more connected, and yet more distinctly personalised.

One outcome of all these developments is that 'lifestyle choice' has become a substitute for the concept of subculture (if not of culture as a whole). Advertising and product development tries to key into lifestyle and demographic shifts, seeing such changes in the market as benign opportunities for increased profit, and continuously trying to engage with the changing desires of the young, the socially mobile, the people most used to the internet-connected computer and the mobile phone as 'domesticated' items, and those with the highest level of disposable income. People under 35 are therefore the focus of attention; they are constantly represented in film and television, and in celebrity culture. And yet media-led moral panics, including those around illegal drug use and binge-drinking (such as the recent phenomenon of the 'bottelin', a type of smart-mob street party in which young Spaniards exchange text messages and emails and then flood into their city centres and drink in public all evening, much to the annoyance of everyone else), also continue to identify young people as a significant social and cultural problem, and to identify the regulation of their behaviour as a social need.

There is a key set of problems here which may increasingly impact on the future of music. It is, apparently, our human right to be distinctively different, to celebrate our lifestyle and sexual choices and religious beliefs without fear, and to join collectively in celebrating the existence of communities of difference. But whereas the legal realisations of the doctrine of individual human rights often include the specified right to live in peace and quiet, there is seldom if ever an equivalent legal right to make any kind of noise – which in effect means that there is no legal right to make music. Addressing this gap will be necessary if live music (and musical innovation of any sort) is to flourish. As it is, the law is continually being brought to bear on this aspect of popular culture in a most unhelpful way.

In March 2004, after extensive consultation, the Mayor of London published an Ambient Noise Strategy. Although the key targets of the strategy focused on transport and industrial noise, the document also referred to 'noisy neighbours' (who had been identified as a particular problem by only four per cent of respondents to the consultation) and pubs and clubs (which were identified as a particular problem by only two per cent of those consulted). The leaflet summarising the new strategy stated baldly that 'Noise makers do not always realise their music systems or other equipment can be confiscated if they repeatedly cause real nuisance'; though it also contained provision for the setting up of a 'London Domestic Noise Fund' to improve insulation against internal and external noise, especially in poorly converted flats, which would seem to indicate that some thought had been given to the ways in which design can provide mutual quiet if needed and/or paid for.[15]

The Mayor's document also warned that:

> In response to global economic and lifestyle trends, parts of London are more active 24 hours a day, seven days a week. Late-night eating, drinking, clubbing and other entertainment, as well as more flexible patterns of living and working, can mean more noise in hitherto quieter periods of the day and week.[16]

The world of advertising and brand development echoed the Mayor's insight. Early in 2005 the UK-based 'brand consultancy' Future Laboratory identified a new woman, who they called HEIDI. The Higher Educated Independent Degree-carrying Individual was, as Future Laboratory saw it, the key customer of this 24-hour urban party lifestyle. According to the consultancy a very remarkable 7.2 million UK-resident individuals could be placed in this demographic niche (the identified male equivalent was the Ladult, who at only 4.2 million was apparently somewhat thinner on the ground). HEIDI was an office worker in her 20s or early 30s, single or with partner but childless. She had reasonable disposable income, and spent all or most of it, often augmenting her earnings with the significant use of credit cards. Her life revolved around play rather than work. 60 per cent of this group identified all-night parties as a normal aspect of weekly life (in other words they went to late-night or all-night events during the week, as well as at the weekend, and if that affected their work performance level, tough luck). The people at Future Laboratory were far too polite to accuse HEIDI of the occasional use of illegal drugs, but they told us that she drank wine in reasonably large quantities, as did her 'elder sister', who they identified as 'Bridget Jones'.

All this makes HEIDI among the most important consumers of urban contemporary and dance music; but providing for her tastes is a legal and social problem. She requires urban venues which can contain serious noise, and if she

---

[15] *The Mayor's Ambient Noise Strategy Highlights*, Mayor of London March 2004, p.1
[16] *The Mayor's Ambient Noise Strategy*, p.8

is to make her full contribution to the economy (buying entrance tickets, food and drink, transport, and night-out clothing) there has to be a licensing structure to facilitate – rather than hinder – the provision of this type of musical entertainment. One aspect of this provision is 24-hour alcohol licensing, which was introduced into the UK for the first time in 2006; but public campaigns against binge-drinking may yet act as a brake on this type of development, and in some towns such licences are unobtainable thanks to public pressure by people who believe they have a 'right' to continuous peace and quiet.

More ordinarily, however, if concert music is to have a future in urban spaces, the problems of noise and neighbours need to be confronted. The first ever purpose-built stadium-sized rock venue in London opens in 2007, using part of the cavernous interior of the Millennium Dome (a resonant space which will be ameliorated, it is to be hoped, by extensively trialled sound-diffusion design). The Dome has the advantage of being relatively isolated from domestic buildings. Even here, though, the process of gaining planning permission for the change of use involved the promise of dual-use during the 2012 Olympic Games, when the venue will host gymnastics and basketball.

A change of name has also helped in the preservation of Britain's premier rock festival. The first Glastonbury festival was held in 1970; now called the Glastonbury Festival of Contemporary Performing Arts, it has become an event of global cultural importance. The event has been held at Worthy Farm in Somerset, a few miles from the town of Glastonbury itself, since 1981, and the event's organisers, led by dairy farmer Michael Eavis, have had recurrent problems with the licensing of the festival. There have been a number of 'fallow years' without a festival, in part to placate the neighbours and the local district council. The last fine for noise was in 2001 when a number of celebrants refused to move on and made loud music for a few days after the official end of the festival.

In other words, late-night parties, festivals and other celebrations had been a perceived legal problem in the UK well before the Mayor of London's strictures were published. In the case of 'acid house', such events led to illiberal changes in the law. In the summer of 1989 a number of free 'acid house' parties were held at empty warehouses in the industrial town of Blackburn, Lancashire, in the north-west of the UK. There was little violence at the events (a lack usually attributed to the effects of the music in conjunction with the use of the drug MDMA or Ecstasy), and so the police did little about them. Nonetheless, the presence of large numbers of young people frightened local residents, the parties were loud, there were clearly health and safety issues in the use of abandoned warehouses, and these factors plus the moral panic about Ecstasy which was orchestrated in the national press at the time led to a campaign to have the parties stopped, supported by all local Members of Parliament (MPs).

Conservative MP Graham Bright's Bill became an Act on 9 March 1990, enabling such parties to be banned. Bright's measures included a new licensing system in which stringent safety regulations were to be enforced by local councils – and these health and safety rules included strict limits on noise levels. These developments (unfavourable reactions from the local media, residents, politicians and warehouse owners, and a new legal framework) changed police behaviour. It was now possible for them lawfully to break up a party, secure prosecution of the organisers and punish them with hefty fines and prison sentences; they did so. No further free warehouse parties have occurred in East Lancashire to date.

This success only encouraged the legislators. A further set of provisions against parties appeared in the 1994 Criminal Justice Act, which became law despite a well organised and highly publicised two-year campaign among dance fans for 'the right to party'. Under the 1994 Act's provisions the police were empowered to arrest anyone gathering in any public space in order to dance to 'music characterised by the emission of a succession of repetitive beats'. There have in fact been few prosecutions under this law; partly because since 1999 the free party scene became less important than licensed venues (though a summer 2006 revival in farmland 'raves' led immediately to punitive police activity).

Perth, in Western Australia, provides another pertinent example of the music/noise/law problem. As with any relatively prosperous city, Perth has a diverse music scene and night-time economy, which has been charted in *Liverpool of the South Seas*, a book edited in 2005 by Tara Brabazon. As part of the 'creative industries', Perth-made musics, which include examples of dance electronica, hip-hop, rock and punk, are seen by Western Australia's government as, in general, worthy of encouragement; but – again, as with most cities – Perth lacks in the provision of venues for dance music parties, or for rock rehearsal and performance. One such venue was the Grosvenor Hotel, a public house which had been a live music venue since the 1980s, using its live room to showcase up-and-coming local bands five nights a week. In 2002 a new resident moved into a building opposite the pub, and – despite having been aware before moving in that the Grosvenor was a live music venue – complained about the noise from the pub. The new resident's complaints continued after the Grosvenor's management had fitted double glazing. Despite a campaign in its favour supported by thousands, in November 2002 the Grosvenor was forced to close as a live music venue.

The new resident had been able to invoke Perth's *Environmental Protection (Noise) Regulations 1997*. Whatever government discourses in favour of the creative industries were in play, they were only words of encouragement rather than legal protection, so the campaigners on behalf of the venue had no comparable legal recourse. As Rebecca Bennett puts it 'Western Australian laws silence not only loud rock music but also the voices and opinions of managers, musicians, bands and fans'[17], and these laws therefore act against Perth being recognised as a major 'talent city' in the same way as Manchester or Seattle have been promoted.

Different approaches are possible. Elsewhere in Australia, in Brisbane, a similar dispute led to the passing of a law which gave existing venues priority over incoming residents, who were assumed to be aware of their existence before moving in. Unless similar legislative measures are taken, music in the city will remain an endangered activity, whatever the Mayor of London (or anyone else) says about the positive aspects of globalisation and 24-hour living.

---

[17] Rebecca Bennett: 'Heritage and Hard Rock: Silencing the Grosvenor Hotel', in *Liverpool of the South Seas. Perth and its Popular Music*, Tara Brabazon (ed.) (University of Western Australia Press 2005) pp.72–80; the quotation identified here is on p.72.

Chapter three

Making music in the digital era: composing, remixing, and performing with machines

The computer as creative tool

While concert performance in hip-hop, rock and pop is still popular, we are now two decades on from the 'acid house' dance music revolution which saw the shift of electronic music from the margins to the mainstream of popular music culture. This and the following two chapters explore two paradoxes. Firstly, in an era when 'creativity' is often invoked as the saviour of both culture and the economy, we explore a creative process which has been in many cases displaced from the body to the machine, and from the composer or performer to the DJ, producer and remixer, and we examine the many ways in which existing music is recycled, remixed, and repackaged. Secondly, even as the ability to store and manipulate and re-use musical information has never been greater (and is increasing), we examine the ways in which the music business has become increasingly jealous of its absolute 'rights' in the ownership of what it identifies as discrete pieces of music, and in which this protective attitude has been countered in turn by further new ways of making and distributing music.

The digital revolution in music is the result of computerisation, which has of course affected almost every aspect of everyday life, but in relation to music the key aspects are the uses of sampling and sequencing in the composition and recording of music; the remixing of existing compositions; and the buying, selling and sharing of music in digital formats.

The beginnings of the transformation of the recording process included the development of electronic instruments such as the voltage-control synthesisers which appeared in the second half of the twentieth century. These first synthesisers were large, expensive and complex instruments with little or no obvious commercial use (they were built by universities for research purposes), but by the mid-1970s there was a range of portable and relatively affordable synthesisers, whether they were cheap keyboard-based instruments such as the Minimoog, or the drum machines developed by companies such as Roland, which used the same voltage-control technology to imitate drum sounds. The ways of generating sounds electronically changed during the 1980s as the analogue voltage control of pitch and timbre was replaced by the digital modelling of sounds, with the Yamaha DX-7 (using a system developed in an American university by the composer John Chowning) leading the field as the first affordable digital synthesiser. The 1980s also saw the appearance of drum machines and synthesisers with built-in 'sequencers' – that is, these instruments could be programmed to play and repeat a short sequence of notes. One immediate result was the cold-sounding electro-pop of bands such as Japan, Human League or the Buggles, or solo artists such as Gary Numan or Howard Jones. Their music is characterised by simple, very precise repeated drum patterns, bass riffs and broken chords, all of which were made on synthesisers and drum machines with sequencers. Subsequently, while the built-in sequencers gained in capacity and flexibility, far greater strides in terms of compositional flexibility were made in the provision of sequencers on computers: these were among the first music composition programmes.

68

In order for this to work effectively the computer had to be able to communicate with the synthesiser or drum machine. After a few years in which manufacturers developed different, incompatible systems, software designers and electronics firms decided to collaborate to produce a common standard. The result, agreed in 1981, was the Musical Instrument Digital Interface (MIDI), which was a control protocol. It allowed any computer or instrument containing the interface to control any other to which it was connected. This meant information about pitch, the strength of attack and decay of an individual note, its timbre and so on could be transmitted in real time for performance (crudely put, one keyboard could control another), or the same information stored in a sequencer – in a computer's or a keyboard instrument's memory – either for the purpose of recording, or replay during live performance.

The second part of the transformation of the recording process was the development of 'sampling', the digital recording of sound. Whereas a traditional tape recorder will record a sound by modelling it in its entirety as a horizontal wave, a sampling device can only sample the sound at one instant and then the next, in a series of vertical cuts. The closer in time these 'cuts' are together, the higher will be the fidelity of the result. While most people would agree that approximately 45,000 samples per second (the standard adopted for CD recording and replay) is as near to the real thing as the human ear can perceive, far higher sampling rates – in other words higher standards of fidelity – are in fact obtainable (and these higher rates have been incorporated into the specifications of the DVD-Audio and Blue-Ray DVD-Video formats). Once sampled, a sound can be played back in real time, or transposed in pitch using any MIDI keyboard, or edited and reshaped using the computer's software, or layered alongside other sounds to produce a more complex timbre – or all of those in combination.

Meanwhile, the recording of music was becoming increasingly computerised, firstly through software written for 'domestic' computers. During the 1980s composition and sequencing programmes were written for machines designed for home and educational use, such as the Commodore 64, the BBC Microcomputer, and especially the Atari ST and the Apple Macintosh. (The Atari and Apple each had a simple graphics-based user interface, and the Atari also had a built-in MIDI connection. The development of an equally intuitive user interface for the IBM PC – Windows – was simply too slow; therefore no-one built a successful dedicated music sequencing system for the PC during the 1980s.)

At a level far more complex and ambitious than the software written for home computers, professional computer-based sampling and sequencing machines were introduced during the early 1980s by the Australian company Fairlight Instruments and the American Synclavier Systems. These instruments were physically big, and difficult to programme; and they were very expensive – costing tens of thousands of dollars. Before the end of the decade, smaller samplers with almost as much memory and processing power as the original Fairlight CMI (Computer Musical Instrument) were available at about one tenth of the cost, and they were far easier to use. Most drum machines by this point also used digital samples of drums rather than the analogue synthesiser technology of the earlier beatboxes (the first drum machine to use actual samples, the Linn Drum, was introduced in 1981). As a result, sampled sounds began to appear in almost all pop, whether recorded or in live performance. All these innovations provided the technological basis for the dance music 'revolution' of the 1980s, from Chicago House and Detroit Techno earlier in the decade through the 'acid house' moment in the Europe of the later 1980s, which remains the basis of the music played in 'superclub' brands such as the Ministry of Sound in the early twenty-first century.

While the new technologies facilitated the new music, it could not have taken off without two significant cultural shifts. Firstly, the Chicago and Detroit clubs where the new minimalist music of repetitive beats and sampled voices was first experienced were largely gay clubs, as were their New York disco-scene forebears; these public venues were the result of the moment of 'gay liberation' in the 1970s, thanks to which the legalisation and/or public toleration of gay sexualities had become commonplace in the USA and Western Europe. Secondly, the Ibiza party scene which helped to launch the UK Acid House movement was the launch-pad of a relentless search for late-night entertainment. Ibiza had been colonised as a multinational holiday resort, with organisations such as Club 18–30 taking young adults away from their routines for relatively cheap fortnight-long holidays based around the physical hedonism of sun, sand, sex, alcohol and other drugs, and parties. People returning from holiday to the UK's poor weather and restrictive licensing laws (which closed bars and pubs at 11 pm) wanted to carry on experiencing all-night entertainment and all-night intoxication, even as the new music's repetitive beats mirrored that mood; and the consumption of the former psychotherapeutic drug Ecstasy, or 'E', was a vital part of the new music experience.

For a while the new dance music was seen as 'faceless' (which worried a music industry built on the grooming of 'stars'); the music was simply there for the dancers' use, and since it was made using machines, then recorded and played over a PA by a DJ, the usual hierarchical relationship between performer and audience was simply unnecessary. All too quickly, however, it became apparent that some DJs could respond to the crowd's mood with particular efficiency, and a number of 'superstar DJs' such as Sasha, Carl Cox, Pete Tong and Fatboy Slim emerged. However, from the start of the dance music 'revolution' there were also 'bands' which tried to provide elements of performance which could not be matched by the booth-bound DJ. There were several different approaches. From slightly to one side of the new music, Manchester-based guitar bands like the Happy Mondays, the Stone Roses and Primal Scream began to play in a more minimalist, repetitive manner clearly influenced by the new dance beats (and the new drugs): the press responded by labelling the new scene 'Madchester'. The next section examines aspects of this musical and cultural transformation in greater detail.

Music inside the dance revolution

Within the dance technologies themselves, Coldcut, and a little later many others on their label Ninja Tune, varied the diet of deckspun and sampled beats at their shows by employing back-projected video images as part of the performance. Coldcut's 1999 double-CD album *Let Us Replay* included free video-editing software which the consumer could use to make their own videos to some of the album's tracks. Meanwhile bands such as Underworld, Ultramarine, The Orb, Prodigy and The Shamen all incorporated the techniques of the new dance music alongside some aspects of live-performance rock styles, in their recordings and live performances. While all these bands used a range of new technologies, it is worth noting the very different ways in which they related to tradition, and to the rest of culture, as well as the technologically new. Underworld, for example, engaged with the 'laddishness' of the football fandom which became newly fashionable after the 1990 World Cup, promoting a cheerfully aggressive but self-aware working-class masculinity (best musically represented, perhaps, in the use of their 1995 track 'Born Slippy' on the final moments of the movie *Trainspotting*); meanwhile the Orb's music deliberately echoed the whimsical middle-class English achievements of progressive rock – achievements which were closely connected with older English musical traditions.

The Orb were not alone. 'When we write songs, we think of landscapes'. That remark is attributed to Ultramarine; it could easily have come from Edward Elgar or Ralph Vaughan Williams, two of the classical composers most closely associated with depictions of the English landscape. In its mid-1990s heyday Ultramarine was a typical hi-tech duo (founders Ian Cooper and Paul Hammond), employing banks of samplers, sequencers and mixers to create layers of trancey, dub-influenced dance music. But their stage act (and recordings) also included live performance, featuring musicians playing guitars, saxes and even a drum kit. The band's first releases, the mini-album *Wyndham Lewis* (1989) and the full-length *Folk* (1990) moved from all-acoustic instrumentation to an acoustic-electronic mix, a shift which was fully announced by the trance rhythms of the second album, *Every Man and Woman is a Star* (1991). The third album, *United Kingdoms* (1993) also displays the vestiges of the traditions of folk and political song. The voice used to sing the songs is that of Robert Wyatt, who first recorded with the jazzy progressive rock band Soft Machine in the late 1960s. Ultramarine's humanisation of techno/dub moved it towards the mainstream which was occupied by bands such as Leftfield, the Chemical Brothers and Underworld, while simultaneously connecting it with that moment of 1960s counter-culture through which a new national popular music emerged. In Ultramarine's music a soundscape is preserved through the sampler as well as through the lived performances of its participants.

71

The Shamen had embodied something similar, moving from folk-rock to techno. Dance-music electronica could not have been further from The Shamen's first incarnation. In the mid-1980s Aberdonian Colin Angus, who was fascinated alike by shamanism – that mix of pharmacologically conferred insight and micropolitical leadership – and by the equally drug-influenced music and lyrics of late-1960s psychedelic rock, formed a band which performed a mix of covers of early Pink Floyd member Syd Barrett's songs, and Barrett-like original songs with obscure and/or political lyrics, in a musical frame of electric and acoustic guitars and drums. These neo-psychedelic values formed the band's sonic signature in their early work for their own Moksha label.

This sound signature was added to in the late 1980s as the first generation of cheap samplers altered popular music's sonic landscape, and the acid house scene produced the first high-profile teenage/young adult subculture since punk. Will Sin, who was at home with the new technologies, began to lead the band in new directions which were confirmed when he and Colin Angus moved to London. Here they met Mr C, a Cockney rapper and DJ, set up The End, a dance club, and produced a series of singles and albums for their new and more pushily commercial label, One Little Indian. These products were deliberately aimed at an indie-rock/pop/dance crossover – the same hybrid musical space which had been negotiated through the 'Madchester' scene of 1989–90. Through live work at their club, The Shamen was able to reinvent its performing skills in the age of the turntable and sequencer, becoming – as did Ultramarine, Underworld, The Prodigy and many others – a dance-rock hybrid, with a stage presence no DJ could match, and indeed with some traditional instruments played in real time, but with musical structures formed by the domination of repetitive, electronically stored and processed rhythm.

Having charted in 1990 with the single 'ProGen', the band appeared to have come to an end when Will Sin drowned, just after the filming of the song's promotional video. Colin Angus eventually decided to carry on, and in 1992 the album *Boss Drum* capitalised on the success of the cheeky single 'Ebenezer Goode'. The latter, with a cheery chorus deliberately subverting the BBC's attempt to ban material referring to illegal drugs, became a number one. The song's trademark pumping bass line and cheesy keyboard sounds, together with Mr C's cheerfully witty rap and the 'Ezer [= Es are] Good' choruses in apparent praise of the rave generation's most important consumable, mark it out as typical of the band's successful hybrid dance-pop. But there's more to the *Boss Drum* album than potential chart pop: it also contains, in 'Re: Evolution', a track which foreshadowed the 'ambient house' of the following years. Over a set of sonically inventive minimalist keyboard riffs, the New Age philosopher Terence McKenna intones a brief version of his basic thesis: that the evolution of human intelligence is due to the ingestion of plants with psychoactive constituents. The shaman, in other words, prefigures the human.

The Shamen's next album, *Axis Mutatis*, provided several variations on these themes – the emphasis was on pop songs using dance technology, with chord changes for choruses alongside repetitive drum patterns and bass lines, and lyrics (delivered through harmony and lead vocals, plus the occasional rap) expressing the band's philosophical and ecological concerns – while for those prepared to pay a little extra, a deluxe version provided *Arbor Bona, Arbor Mala*, a second CD of mixes of the same material, mostly without featured vocals. This bonus album revealed the extent of the band's continuing interaction with the dance culture and its proliferating subgenres. Likewise, a number of extended-play 'single' CDs of tracks drawn from the album showed the same material mixed in house, garage, hardcore techno, and drum'n'bass styles, by a number of the scene's leading producers and performers. Having reinvented performance, in releasing this plethora of mixes The Shamen had embraced totally the new musical concept of the 1990s and after: that there is no finished, 'authentic' version of a song or track. Any piece of digitally recorded music was just material which could and should be varied infinitely by those coming into contact with it.

The band had already by this point established a strong and innovative presence on the internet. They had launched albums and singles, and uploaded clips of music and video for fans to use well before this became the marketing norm. Several times they broadcast live performances to their Nemeton website, for the worldwide fanbase to enjoy for free. Their next album,

Hempton Manor, had its own witty pro-cannabis (hemp) web pages. But this album, a series of 'instrumentals' which according to Angus had been planned, programmed, recorded and mixed in less than a week, did not please the people at the record label, who were hoping for more chart singles. One Little Indian released some material, including a couple of remixes, without The Shamen's permission. The band left One Little Indian and returned to Moksha, releasing a final CD, *UV*, a survey both of the band's own evolution and of the history of dance music since the Acid House revolution of the late 1980s.

The Shamen had come a long way from those semi-acoustic covers of songs by Syd Barrett, but they were to go no further. Having released *UV* and its associated singles, and made a last performing appearance, somewhat bizarrely, on a television show hosted by celebrity presenter Melinda Messenger, The Shamen announced that they had decided to devote their future activities to what they saw as the communications medium of the future. Early in 1999 a press release announced that The Shamen would cease to perform live; they were going to reinvent themselves as a 'virtual' band, with no further live work or commercially released albums. In future all their music would be created and disseminated electronically, as would all communication with them, which would centre around their web page, Nemeton. The press release concluded that the band would be 'reformatted' in virtual space, and would be in touch with fans in due course. But there were no such communications: nothing further happened. Colin Angus apparently returned to study, and Mr C went back to The End. The Shamen did not, in fact, have a virtual future.

This does not mean that a 'virtual band' is an impossibility. The Beatles after all had retired from live performance in the mid-1960s, and carried on for another five years; twenty years later the KLF and Future Sound of London had also pioneered a shadowy existence with various forms of hybrid internet, video and radio-based performance, and one of the most innovative and commercially successful acts of the early twenty-first century was Gorillaz, who have released two successful CD and DVD albums so far, including a 'live' album. It would seem that unlike the manufactured pop acts of the 1990s boy/girl bands or the products of reality television shows such as *American Idol*, Gorillaz are as their name might suggest the genuine Monkees of the new millennium, the true inheritors of that moment of 1960s madness. One key difference from the reality television charm-school graduates who festoon reality television might be the relatively well-known personnel of Gorillaz, which is led by former Blur vocalist and frontman Damon Albarn. Another is the expensive website and cartoon videos which place them at the forefront of audio-visual entertainment. Live shows reinforce the 'virtuality' of the Gorillaz themselves by placing the band's front-line singers and musicians behind a screen, while their backing singers and musicians perform in full view; meanwhile the cartoons and associated images are projected onto the screen.

The computer as creative *partner*

In all the music discussed so far the computer has been used as a substitute for recording tape, sound effects processing and the mixing desk. It has become more proficient at these tasks. As onboard memory and processing speeds have increased, music programmes have become able to record instrumental and vocal performances in real time as well as storing sequencing information. The same programmes offer facilities for correction, editing, and 'perfecting', (including the manipulation of inadequate performances). Exquisitely small fractions of time and pitch can be changed.

Other modes of composition also allow the computer a more 'creative' role, which in a way harks back to the experimental approaches taken by two modernist 'classical' composers who were at work in the late 1950s and early 1960s. The American John Cage escaped from the Western tradition of composition by turning to a deliberate indeterminacy, while Karlheinz Stockhausen sought refuge from the terrifying political legacy of German romanticism in the rigours of mathematics and the new disciplines of the recording studio, producing music in which pitch, rhythm and timbre alike were subject to arithmetical procedures, rather than any aesthetic of sensuous expression. The computer *can* also be the generator of aleatoric processes which involve some level of 'composition' by the machine itself. The Koan software programme, for example, will produce music according to the user's specifications in a somewhat Cagean manner, while programmes such as the Composers Desktop Project (hosted at the UK's York University) allow for mathematical rigour in individual sound processing as well as the larger-scale aspects of composition.

Such approaches are also part of the development of popular music. Take for example the extreme 'post-dance' music of Rob Booth and Sean Brown, a.k.a. Autechre, who represent the flowering of a new kind of musicianship in the digital era. Before the 1980s most musicality was expressed through the voice or through instrumental proficiency which was learned either through listening and copying or some more formal education structure. Stockhausen's music-lab experiments were copied by a few, and had little early influence in popular music. The people who formed Ultramarine and The Shamen were typical rock-era instrumentalists who grew towards the techniques and technologies of dance music composition from more orthodox performing and song writing. Similarly, classically trained musicians such as Prodigy's Liam Howlett, or the American trance-musician-turned-film-composer BT (whose film score credits include the Rob Cohen movies *The Fast and the Furious* (2001) and *Stealth* (2005)), came to electronica and the computer keyboard after having learned conventional piano-keyboard skills. The obvious variation on this rule was hip-hop, whose artists from the late 1970s onwards pioneered the use of small, cheap drum machines, and vinyl records spun on turntables, to provide loops of sound to accompany the rappers' work.

Booth and Brown were neither trained nor self-taught as acoustic instrumentalists but learned their craft in the late 1980s through a musicality more akin to hip-hop, experimenting with the production of new sounds through the manipulation of tape decks, record decks and computers. Early adopters of computer software for sampling, sequencing and the manipulation of sound, in the early 1990s Autechre began to release a sequence of CDs, CD singles and EPs, and DVDs on the Sheffield-based Warp label (which is also home to the somewhat more musically conventional Aphex Twin and Squarepusher). The duo's CD sleeve designs, like some of the recordings, are forbiddingly abstract, with no human imagery and little or no information beyond track titles. While the music was in the earliest releases recognisably based on electronic dance music, it has become starker and less easy to follow, as it strips down and rebuilds rhythmic structures without any concession to the idea of actual dancing, or to conventional ideas of tonal harmony for that matter. Autechre write their own composition software, and often use mathematical procedures for the initiation of tracks – which means that the mechanical (and easily recognisable) repetition of beats which can be found in their early work is lost as the programme generates its own rules for the building of rhythms, and the composers respond by isolating, combining and mixing the results as they see fit.

Music with this level of abstraction is relatively rare even within what could be called the Warp end of the dance music world. The equally rebarbative sounds made by the Finnish duo Pan Sonic, for example, are usually organised into more easily recognisable rhythmic structures. But like Autechre, Pan Sonic are not traditionally trained musicians but ground-up experimenters with the fundamentals of sound generation, using microphones, jack lead inputs and amplifiers as creatively as they use the more sophisticated software and hardware of the recording studio and its compact computerised equivalents. Compared with Pan Sonic's and Autechre's, the electronic output of the Prodigy and BT sounds relatively conventional; BT's 1990s trance albums, such as ima (1995) have even been likened to romantic classical compositions – one reviewer described this album as 'fairy-tale symphonies', and was quoted as such on the album cover. By this standard Pan Sonic, Autechre and many others produce genuinely new music.

Sound is money

The creative industries depend on recycling, and they also depend on the control of copyright and intellectual property. However, legal and ethical debates about copyright often ignore the copying of *sound*, which is a fundamental part of the making of music. Copying identifiable patterns of rhythm and melody is clearly illegal in most cases, but though some commentators have proposed the idea of the 'soundmark' as opposed to the currently copyrightable aspects of melody and harmony, copying the soundworlds made by composers or artists is at present less obviously a breach of copyright than copying actual recorded sounds, or pitch and rhythmic relationships which could be written as a score.

This is a matter of convention, and there are others: for example, in the USA it is unusual to pay performer royalties on subsequent sales of recordings, while in the UK it is customary, and the British courts have therefore generated a number of interesting cases involving performers' rights. But in each country there are public disputes about the ownership of soundworlds – often because of changes in personnel among bands which have made recordings. Many long-lasting bands have had changes in key personnel: the Rolling Stones, for example, are still organised around three of the original five core members, but have changed their second guitarist twice since Brian Jones's departure (and subsequent death) in 1969; and they've gigged and recorded since 1992 with 'guest' bass players. Original bassist Bill Wyman's exit from the Stones was relatively friendly, but many of these changes in personnel have been acrimonious, and the resulting debates, rivalries and legal arguments – among members and former members of for example Pink Floyd, The Fall, Yes, and Red Hot Chili Peppers – often question the relationship between personnel, the name or brand-name of the band, and the resulting sound.

In March 2006, at a ceremony in Memphis, Blondie was inducted into the Rock and Roll Hall of Fame. As the band's current line-up waited on stage to play a celebratory song, two former members of the band (bassist Nigel Harrison and guitarist Frank Infante) stood up and started to shout that they, too, should be included since they were part of the 'real' Blondie, c.1976–82, and as such, though they did not claim credit as composers, their sonic input had helped to create the band's trademark clean but angsty post-punk sound on its most successful singles such as 'Heart of Glass'. Harrison and Infante had briefed some members of the press beforehand, and they had even, thoughtfully, brought their instruments with them, though in the end bandleaders and founder-members Deborah Harry and Chris Stein did not invite them to join them onstage.

The first Oasis drummer, Tony McCaroll, was sacked from the band in early 1995 after the recording of the band's first album, *Definitely Maybe*. McCaroll sued for compensation for loss of future earnings in 1999, his lawyers arguing that he had been part of a band which, as a partnership, had been offered a five-album deal. The court recognised that the recording contract had indeed been offered to a partnership, but as the partnership had no written agreement he had in fact been vulnerable to expulsion. But the legal arguments also included the question of the band's trademark sound, and whether or not McCaroll had contributed to it. The remaining members of the band opined in court that he had been a poor drummer who made little effort to improve, that his efforts in the recording studio had had very little to do with the band's success, and that he had been sacked for these, musical, reasons, rather than for the 'personality differences' which had been mooted by tabloid newspapers. The courts sympathised with McCaroll, who was awarded about £500,000.

Similar disputes have arisen between session musicians and their star employers. For example, in the early 1980s Martin Dobson was a session musician who regularly worked with Annie Lennox and Dave Stewart, also known as the Eurythmics. Dobson played a prominent baritone sax part – including a recognisable repeated riff and an improvised solo – on 'Right by Your Side', the third single taken from the 1983 Eurythmics album *Touch*; he was paid his usual fee for the performance. The single was a worldwide hit, and Dobson asked for composer royalties. His lawyers argued, against fierce opposition from the legal representatives of Stewart and Lennox, that his riff, his improvisation, and the distinctive sound of his sax playing entitled him to a composition credit on the song, and therefore to increased royalties. The courts agreed with him.

The legal cases involving tracks on the first two albums by Enigma raise a number of more complex issues about soundworld and copyright. In 1992 *MCMXC A.D.* was released on the Virgin label. Under the band name Enigma, the album featured the work of the Romanian musician Michael Cretu, also known as Curly M.C., as composer and leading performer, with a Germany-based production team which included Frank Peterson, also known as Frank Gregorian. 'Sadeness', the first single taken from the album, became a global hit single. This track featured a distinctive sound signature: breakbeat rhythm loops, long-sustained synthesiser chords slowly changing in timbre, a melody line played by a sampled shakuhachi (a Japanese wooden flute with a breathy and wistful quality), female spoken voice and lead vocals, and – most strikingly – a sampled male voice choir, synchronised to the rhythm track, singing Gregorian chant in Latin. Enigma's original publicity claimed that the chanters were a Romanian choir. As it happens, the choir involved was the German ensemble Kapelle Antiqua, and having recognised its work the choir was unimpressed by Enigma's version of events, and sued; the out-of-court settlement included payments to the choir and to Polydor and BMG, two record labels which had licensed Kapelle Antiqua's recordings.[18]

---

18 Much more detail on this part of the story can be found in Timothy Taylor's *Strange Sounds. Music, Technology and Culture* (Routledge 2001) pp.232–8.

The global success of 'Sadeness' stimulated widespread interest in Gregorian chant, and in medieval music more widely. In 1994, for example, a double CD, *Canto Gregoriano*, crossed over from the fledgling classical music chart and entered the mainstream UK pop album chart, while at the same time the 'classical' chart featured *Officium*, an album on the ECM label on which saxophonist Jan Garbarek improvised to the accompaniment of medieval liturgical music provided by the Hilliard Ensemble. Nonetheless, Enigma's next move left the medieval world behind, but involved a rather different form of ethically dubious sampling.

Perhaps in order to avoid more legal difficulties *Cross of Changes*, the follow-up to *MCMXC A.D.*, used samples from ethnographic field recordings – material which is apparently in the public domain, but which, while often valuably documenting traditional performance, tends not to reward performers beyond crediting their work. The *Cross of Changes* album's most successful single was 'Return to Innocence', which used, among other sources, sampled traditional music of the Taiwanese aboriginal tribe the Ami, performed by two Ami singers, Kuo Hsiu-Chu and her husband Kuo Ying-Nan. The sample was taken from a public-domain recording of traditional Taiwanese music, for the use of which Enigma had paid a fee. Thanks to the use of 'Return to Innocence' in a promotional video for the 1996 Atlanta Olympic Games, the Kuos found out about their unwitting contribution, and sued, in the end reaching another out-of-court settlement which included naming the Kuos in future album packaging.[19]

Michel Cretu, who his advisers and fans alike construct as an originating musical 'genius', meanwhile systematically refuses to list all the samples used in Enigma recordings which are the sources for his original/transformative work. The originators of these sounds and rhythms therefore – unless they can follow the Kuos' example – remain uncredited, whether or not they are financially rewarded. Cretu's publishers, Mambo Musik, claim that this denial of what would seem to be the basic rights of any recording artist, to have the sounds they make acknowledged in publication details, is to prevent others from cashing in by copying their artist's original and creative use of such recordings and making mere pastiches of the Enigma sound.

This is perhaps an understandable position, but it is in this instance odd,

---

[19] Kuo Ying-Nan used this money to finance an album under his own name, *Circle of Life*. The album was not of traditional Ami music as such but of his own, dare we say it, Enigma-style take on the postmodern roots sound, featuring traditional vocal and instrumental material backed up by breakbeats and washes of synthesiser sound: the sampled artist had in turn copied the Enigma soundworld.

because the Enigma *sound* was in fact systematically, and very successfully, copied, in another follow-up to the first Enigma album which has become a long-running phenomenon in its own right. Enigma producer Frank Peterson came up with a project he called Gregorian. He hired a male voice choir, consisting of men schooled in opera and/or the Anglican choral tradition, to sing Gregorian-chant-style arrangements of classic pop songs from the Anglo-American repertoire (with the familiar lyrics sung in English, not Latin). The arrangements also featured a sound signature which any fan of Enigma would have found familiar: breakbeats providing the drum patterns, synthesised bass lines, gently washing synthesiser chords, solo female lead vocals, and at times even sampled melodies which apparently use the exact shakuhachi sample featured on 'Sadeness'. This is a late 1980s 'factory sample' which was provided by Akai for use with their samplers such as the S1000 model. Akai's sample of the shakuhachi has a characteristic swooping glitch towards the end of the note (despite which it, too, is not credited to a named performer). The result, for Peterson at least, was happiness: the first Gregorian album, *Masters of Chant*, released in 1999, achieved gold status in sixteen countries including Germany, South Africa, Australia and Singapore. Gregorian has at the time of writing produced five CD albums, a greatest hits collection, and a live concert DVD, and their 'sound signature' in turn helped to create space for the much darker German 'electro-medieval' band Helium Vola, founded in 2001, which performs songs in impeccable Latin and medieval German. I am not aware of any legal dispute over the copied sound signature – perhaps because Peterson could claim that the Enigma sound was in part his own intellectual property – but a Gregorian track like that first album's 'Still I'm Sad' is on the face of it at least as much an infringement of creative originality as Enigma's own use of unwitting monkish choirs or Taiwanese singers.

There is, it seems, little or no ethical or legal debate about Gregorian's recreation of Enigma's soundworld, or of Helium Vola's development of it, since custom and practice involves listening to and mimicking the sounds of existing musical practices as the principal mode of transmission in popular music's 'oral culture'. Indeed, the copying of looks and sounds *has* to be possible, otherwise there would be no genres, and nothing to sell as such; to this extent the music business and the public alike are happy to collude in accepting the routine sameness of most musics, while the music business would continue to insist that the originality and authorship it promotes as the basis of differentiable 'rights' are based on minor differences in melody or harmony, rather than in say timbre, tempo or timeframe. Despite the possibilities offered by the digital world, copyright remains wedded to traditional Western notions of musical originality.

Chapter four

Buying and selling music in the digital era: recycling and remaking

There is more music available to more people in more formats than ever before. But much of this is not actually new music. Old recordings are continually recycled within radio formats or in repackaged CDs, and as this happens groupings of 'classic' tracks emerge. They might be associated with specific performers, or genres, or even decades, but their presence, and their number, increases as time passes. All those performing and composing in any genres of music, and their fans, and those who wish to stimulate music sales, now have to find ways of dealing with the increasing archive of available recorded music. They are doing so in different ways, though in a sense what is happening in classical, jazz, rock and pop looks very like convergence. Classical music is increasingly marketed in the same ways as pop, but still the music of the nineteenth century is valued more highly than new compositions (unless they sound rather like nineteenth-century music, as many Hollywood film scores do). American jazz has arguably become a set of learned techniques rather than a space for continual innovation. Pop music is increasingly concerned with style revivals, covers and tribute bands, in other words with reproducing its own past while still introducing new artists. Meanwhile a lot of music is also being made from the fragments of the old, and this new mode of composition and arranging is another way of dealing with the weight of the musical past. The next two chapters explore aspects of the survival and revival strategies of classical, rock and even dance music – which is now a mature genre in its twenties, and with a history of its own.

Classical music becomes pop... and the opera goes to Glastonbury

Classical music became pop during and after the 1980s. The last quarter of the twentieth century saw the deaths of a generation of great orchestral conductors – notably Leonard Bernstein, Herbert von Karajan, and Sir Georg Solti. Much of the prestige of classical music recording had been quite literally embodied by these figures, who were successful sellers and earners. At the time of his death in July 1989 Herbert von Karajan had sold 115 million albums for the Deutsche Grammophon (DG) label, and tens of millions more for two other labels, Decca and EMI. While he and the other conductors had been marketed as superstars, often with their name and the name of the composer whose work they had recorded receiving joint billing on album covers, they were leading a project which gave the wishes of the composers the utmost respect. The composer's work was usually represented in full even when that meant at great length and cost, with both Solti and von Karajan recording complete versions of Wagner's *Ring of the Nibelung* opera cycle (which has about fourteen hours of music in total, and needs expensive resources including a very large orchestra, a chorus, and singers at the peak of their physical powers for the principal roles) and the record companies making every effort to market the result. Bernstein often recorded complex and difficult contemporary music, some of it his own, and he likewise received the full support of his record label, Columbia, in doing so.

This seriousness was not *always* enthusiastically endorsed by the record labels, however, and their efforts to increase the commodity status of classical music increased during the 1990s. The DG label made some money in 1995 with *Karajan Adagio*, a CD collection of slow and potentially sentimental moments from music by Mahler, Mozart, Brahms and other composers; the collection was succeeded in the following year by the inventively titled *Karajan Adagio 2*. It's probable that the label had only managed to carry out this particular piece of repackaging because Herbert von Karajan was safely dead. When DG proposed to follow this success with a CD of slow movements from Mahler symphonies, taken from a complete set of the symphonies conducted by Claudio Abbado, the conductor, still very much alive, angrily refused to sanction the procedure. Abbado insisted that consumers should have the opportunity to listen to the music in the sequence the composer had intended.

This repackaging was possible partly because of an opera revival in the late 1980s. Ticket sales increased as more people with money to spend chose a night at the opera as a form of conspicuous consumption. In response to this phenomenon of relatively 'popular opera', the BBC chose as their theme tune for broadcasts from the 1990 football World Cup, which was held in Italy, a recording of the aria 'Nessun Dorma' from Puccini's *Turandot*, sung by the Italian tenor Luciano Pavarotti. A concurrent single release of Pavarotti's rendition of this aria reached number two in the British pop charts. Cashing in on the moment, a concert by the world's three leading tenors, Pavarotti, Placido Domingo and Jose Carreras, was broadcast globally live from Rome on the eve of the World Cup final. The broadcast reaped massive sales in television rights, and video and CD follow-up recordings. The phenomenon was repeated note for note (in both senses) during the next World Cup, which was held in the USA in 1994.

It is interesting to compare the Three Tenors phenomenon with the recorded output of the 'three great conductors'. In each case what was on offer was commercially successful – in other words, music from within the European classical tradition was fuelling the commercial modernity of the global leisure industry – but increasingly this was on the leisure industry's terms. The Three Tenors were *Karajan Adagio* in live performance, but dumbed-down a bit more:

they sang bite-size chunks of opera alongside songs from musicals and popular songs from various European countries. This was not 'classical music' in the sense which would have been recognised by the older generation of conductors. It was, quite deliberately, turning some aspects of the classical repertoire into popular music.

In Britain, the next stage in this process was a significant change in broadcasting. Radio station Classic FM won a licence as part of a government-run competition for new commercial radio stations (among the other winners was the former pirate radio station Kiss FM, which became the first legitimate dance-music radio channel). Classic FM started to broadcast in 1992. It almost immediately found an audience big enough to please its advertisers, its regular listening base overtaking the BBC's existing channel dedicated to classical music, Radio Three, within six months; by early 1994 it boasted 4.5 million listeners weekly, against Radio Three's claimed 2.75 million. Classic FM did this by reversing the careful policy in which Radio Three made every effort to respect what it assumed was the composer's intentions. Radio Three broadcast complete works with no breaks; its announcers provided detailed information about the composers and artists (usually assuming that the listener already had a great deal of basic knowledge about the repertoire) and hardly anything else beyond occasional summaries of news and weather. There was relatively little on-air interaction with the listening public. A weekly review of new recordings, which included a great deal of scholarly comparison, was as close as the channel came to acknowledging the commodity status of music.

Classic FM did not play complete works but excerpts; it did not employ 'announcers' but DJs, who provided jokey comments, and, increasingly, interacted on-air with listeners' telephone calls, text messages and emails. They were usually enthusiastic about the music they were playing, but they did not give the impression that they knew much more about it than the assumed listener. There were breaks for advertisements. The station took it for granted that music was a commodity, to be bought and sold. Classical sales charts were broadcast (and were often dominated by recently released orchestral film scores rather than what Radio Three would have recognised as classical music), and these classical charts were celebrated by a weekly rundown programme. This weekly chart show was at first presided over by Paul Gambaccini, an experienced radio DJ who had for many years also delivered the pop chart show for the BBC's pop station Radio One. Furthermore, at exactly the same time that pop was turning away from the single-artist album and towards the concept-packaging of collections of tracks (the 'compilation album'), Classic FM promoted compilation albums such as *Classics from the Ads, Turbo Classics* (for driving) and *Classics for Lovers*, all marketed under the soothing general soubriquet of 'the world's most beautiful music'. Classical music had indeed become pop.

Radio Three responded partly by playing more well-known music during the daytime (though complete rather than in excerpts); partly by using friendlier-sounding announcers; and partly by developing a far wider sense of its own obligations to the whole non-pop musical ecology, increasingly seeing its mission as including the preservation of jazz, and traditional musics from all over the world, alongside what it saw as the chief threatened species such as new and 'difficult' classical music. Classic FM had changed Radio Three, and in doing so it had changed the way in which this defender of 'the best' in music thought about music itself.

At one level there was strong convergence. Each station launched a magazine. True to form, *BBC Music* featured a front-cover CD of one or more complete performances, whether specially recorded or from its archive, while the *Classic FM Magazine*'s cover CD was a commercial promotion: a selection of excerpted items from new and recent commercial releases. However, once inside the glossy front covers the contents of the publications were very similar – interviews with artists, reviews of recordings, and chatty, introductory features on even the best-known music and musicians from the classical tradition. The comparison with *The Listener*, which had offered genuinely critical responses to the BBC's broadcast output before its closure in 1976, was stark. The new magazines were aimed at people who knew little or nothing of classical music.

A book published under the byline of Classic FM, *Stephen Fry's Incomplete and Utter History of Classical Music, as told to Tim Lihoreau* underlines the missionary intentions of the Classic FM project. The book presents a relentlessly comic (if not actually very funny) version of the lives and works of the great composers, with popular music as the constant frame of reference. For example, when describing the state of play in Europe in 1796, the authors tell us that:

> The wedding of the year has got to have been that of Napoleon Bonaparte to Josephine de Beauharnais – she of 'not tonight' fame... But musically, where were we? Who's the ageing Status Quo type, who's the youthful S Club Seven-ers? Well, the smart money is on twenty-six year old Beethoven to come up with something fantastic following last year's impressive opus 1, *Three Piano Trios*. Would he be a U2 or a Sigue Sigue Sputnik?[20]

Though it's full of this type of knowing reference to pop, rock and soul (which implies that the reader knows a great deal about this music already, and is only just beginning to learn about the classical stuff – if they don't know about pop

---

[20] Stephen Fry's *Incomplete and Utter History of Classical Music, as told to Tim Lihoreau* (Pan 2005) p.108

and rock, they won't get the jokes), very typically for the Classic FM project the book glosses over the difficulty for audiences of much twentieth-century composed music, partly by ignoring it, partly by claiming that film scores are the real classical music of our times.

So in many ways classical music was marketed as pop. We shouldn't be surprised then that from the late 1980s on this music was sold using sex, and especially the sexual allure of young women such as the singers Ute Lemper and Cecilia Bartoli, violinists Sarah Chang and Leila Josefowicz, and cellist Ofra Harnoy (male violinist Nigel Kennedy, by contrast, was represented as a 'lad', complete with punky spiked hair, football fan's scarf, and an irreverent attitude expressed in a cockney accent). Perhaps the most controversial of these treatments was of another violinist, Vanessa-Mae, whose first 'pop' single, released in 1995 (an arrangement by Mike Batt of music by Bach), was advertised with a promotional video in which this very young, very slim woman was seen emerging from water enveloped only in a translucent dress; an erotic image verging on the paedophile.

A few years later, in 1998, the 12-year-old Welsh singer Charlotte Church made a successful album, and thankfully she was not eroticised at this point – instead the album was titled *The Voice of an Angel*. Two further albums reinforced this sense of talented innocence. However, in 2002, *when she was still only 16,* Charlotte Church was given a ludicrous award as the possessor of 'the rear of the year'. Needless to say a great deal of licentious coverage about her body followed in the popular press. Church's subsequent decision to go with the flow and to attempt to re-launch herself as a very un-angelic rock singer makes perfect sense in this context. As the title implies, *Tissues and Issues* (2005), the first Charlotte Church rock album, includes a number of acrid reflections on the artist's very individual experiences of the problems of teenagehood.

For Charlotte Church, having been one thing, was now very definitely the other; but elsewhere in the world of highly commodified 'classical music' there were doubts and anxieties over the nature and classification of the product. Also, still controversially, there was and is crossover with pop among some well-trained performers on classical instruments; others tried to inhabit both worlds. Crossover classical-pop fusion was an emergent category in the early years of the twenty-first century. Instrumentalists and singers trained to conservatory standard but performing a mix of easy listening classical excerpts and new compositions in romantic or sentimental styles, and orchestras performing film music or computer game scores, have marked the emergence of the new crossover genre – even though once again it is often classified for sales purposes as 'classical music'.

There are, however blurred, limits to the classification. The two key questions for the guardians of classical music, such as critics and concert promoters, were firstly, is, say, a Vivaldi concerto played on an electric violin with synthesiser accompaniment actually classical music? And secondly, if so, was the performer any good at playing it, as opposed to good-looking while playing it? Many from the orthodox classical music press refused to give Vanessa-Mae any credit as a performer. Her management's decision to set up in 1997 a Vanessa-Mae 'classical tour' (complete with a sixteen-piece chamber orchestra, but otherwise with all the trappings of the major rock tour) did not solve the problem: if anything it reinforced this sense that she was simply a good-looking young pop star who happened to play the violin.

There was similar controversy over the all-young-female string quartet Bond, which leading operatic baritone Sir Thomas Allen castigated in 2002 as being part of the dumbing-down of classical music. He need not have worried; as he should have known, well before the time of his rant Bond's first album, *Born* (2000), had in fact been considered to have crossed all the way over to pop, and – with the usual blaze of free publicity – it was solemnly banned from the classical charts. Bond is among the 'classical' projects undertaken by the eminent light music composer Mike Batt, who had done most of the composition and arranging for Vanessa-Mae's first album *The Violin Player* (1995). Batt's many credits as composer, manager, producer and talent developer also include classical-fusion chamber ensemble The Planets, as well as the comic 1970s pop group the Wombles and, more recently, jazzy singer-songwriter Katie Melua.

The Wombles wore masks and costumes on stage, but all the other performers in the Batt cave are young-looking and telegenic as well as reasonably capable performers. So are the star male singers of this 'crossover' genre, notably Andrea Bocelli, Russell Watson, and Il Divo, who have been described not unfairly as a 'classical boy band'. Following the example of the Three Tenors, and considerably younger, more handsome and well-groomed, their music is described as 'operatic arrangements of pop songs'. Their Svengali is pop manager and operator Simon Cowell, whose previous achievements include the very unoperatic boy bands Westlife and Five, and who also deserves co-instigation credit for the *Pop Idol* global television franchise (on which he appeared as a self-caricaturing, acidic and opinionated critic in both the UK and USA – *American Idol* – versions of the show). *Ancora*, the second album by Il Divo, topped not the classical but the pop chart in mid-November 2005.

Not all attempts to broadcast the beauties of classical music or the classically trained voice were as naively populist as this wretched essay in dumbing-down. The first Glastonbury festival opera performance was a gig by the English National Opera in 2004. The company rendered the entire, 80-minute third act of Wagner's opera *Die Walküre*. There was nothing dumb about this performance, or about the music itself. The act begins with the sequence 'The Ride of the Valkyries' (perhaps best known from its use in the film *Apocalypse Now*, directed by Francis Ford Coppola in 1979); subsequently there is a series of long and relatively undramatic dialogues and monologues. Though it isn't exactly easy listening, perhaps this hefty chunk of Wagner was a more obvious choice for the Glastonbury festival's first taste of opera than a similar stretch of Mozart or Puccini might have been. Through the mass exposure of every generation since the 1960s to the work of Tolkien, there are very strong links between the Northern European myth-world of Wagner's Ring operas, and the romanticism of rock – heavy metal acts worldwide from the Canadian trio Rush to the Finnish band Sonata Arctica play with this imagery. Whether or not the audience made such connections, the performance was watched attentively and appreciatively by a crowd of some 15,000, ten per cent of the approximately 150,000 in attendance at the festival that year, and five times more than the crowd which would have been able to see a single performance of the work within the English National Opera's home, the Coliseum in central London.

This innovation acknowledges the widening of the Glastonbury demographic. Many people have been going to these events on and off since they started in the 1970s; the rock generation and its punk, indie, grunge, dance and post-dance children and grandchildren have learned to mingle together reasonably happily. It isn't just a rock festival anymore; the renaming of the event as a 'festival of the performing arts' means that as well as catering for more than just music, it also makes more serious attempts to cater for adults, including those with families, as well as young people. The first dedicated festival family camping space opened in 2000, and it has been heavily booked ever since. Older people are significantly more likely to have broadened their taste to include music from the classical tradition. Classic FM, for example, relies on a continuous wave of new converts to the easy-listening aspects of this music tradition from the ageing population.

As they do at Glastonbury, families also mingle at many other outdoor events round the world which focus on (light) classical music. There are numerous James Bond evenings and Three Tenors-type events, and 'the last night of the proms' has become a global franchise. All over the UK orchestras play in the gardens of country houses such as Herstmonceux Castle, Longleat, and Petworth, under the general soubriquet Last Night of the Proms; on the actual last night of the BBC's festival, there are dispersed versions of the event hosted by the Corporation's Welsh, Scottish, Northern English and Northern Irish orchestras, in many cases with guest appearances by local rock and pop musicians. But the phenomenon is far wider than the UK. Since the mid-1980s the Belgian promoters Prommusic have taken a classical orchestra plus mainstream Anglo-American soul and rock performers such as Al Jarreau,

Texas, and Bryan Ferry to a number of venues in France, Spain, Germany, Belgium, Switzerland and Holland for similar outdoor celebrations. The 'patriotic' English music of Sir Edward Elgar is always the centre-point of these evenings, in an event-genre which has become so everyday-popular in Continental Europe that in 1994 one German political party even adopted the slow melody from Elgar's Pomp and Circumstance March no. 1, 'Land of Hope and Glory', as a theme tune for an election campaign.

88 Popular music becomes 'classical'; or, the rise and rise of the tribute band

In adopting and adapting the Last Night of the Proms format, Prommusic have played their part in the commercialisation of classical music and its reinvention as a form of light music aimed at people over 40. But the taste of the over-40s is always changing. The current generation of over-40s have lived through much of the history of pop and rock'n'roll, and radio formats such as Jack, AOR, and Gold FM have reflected this key demographic shift. In Britain the 'light music' of small orchestras, brass bands and choral societies has largely been displaced from 'easy listening' radio formats, which now offer rock, soul and pop – the BBC's Radio Two, for example, has largely reinvented itself for the mature rock generation since the mid-1990s, and the station's listening figures have been on an upward trend ever since. Meanwhile in the autumn of 2006 the BBC inaugurated what it hopes will be a new annual event, the 'electric proms'. Though there was a range of genres, and some new artists were represented, in the main the event featured artists whose musical prime occurred from the 1960s to1990s, including The Who, James Brown (in one of his final public appearances), Paul Weller, Jamiroquai and Fatboy Slim.

In a very simple sense, then, popular music is increasingly dominated by its own history. This has been a developing trend for quite a while, and perhaps began as the music business sought to capitalise on its back catalogues. Mono recordings from the 1920s to the 1950s were being remastered in an unconvincing 'electronic stereo' format in the late 1960s. The repackaging of 'classic' rock albums started in the 1970s; this tendency was given a significant upward push by the early 1980s arrival of CD and the subsequent reformatting and remastering strategies which it was claimed refreshed the original recordings. With the increasing presence of recordings from the past in new formats, radio, TV and print criticism evolved a response, some of which was quite serious history (for example the Ken Burns television series on jazz in the USA, and its UK equivalents *Jazz Britannia, Soul Britannia* and *Folk Britannia*). As usual, however, though they make every effort to present various forms of popular music within a wide frame of reference, such scholarly surveys tend to leave commercial pop music out of the picture; the historicisation of chart pop is therefore led by a variety of 'greatest hits' formats and quiz-show trivia.

Pop's own sense of history is indeed expressed through chatty television shows and websites, and the equivalent magazines. But it also has a 'living history' of cover and tribute bands, through which music fans of any age can 'access all eras'. Indeed, the latter tendency is often reflected in the booking policies of pubs and larger venues. Here for example is the May 2006 line-up of music events at a 600-place venue, The Brook, in the Southern English port city of Southampton:

- Coldplay tribute band
- Midge Ure, formerly of Ultravox
- T. Rex tribute band
- Rory Gallagher tribute band
- Green Day tribute band
- Local DJ
- A non-tribute band who are described as playing 'Moody, Floydian Celtic-tinged rock'
- Local soul band which will play music from movies *The Blues Brothers* and *The Commitments*
- Bob Marley tribute band
- A '70s-style funk band' which will perform music by Kool and the Gang, Barry White, James Brown, and KC and the Sunshine band.

The 'meaning' of the tribute band seems to have two complementary aspects. Firstly, rock, soul and pop have been around for a long while, and fans, critics and the music business have combined to build the story of popular music since the watershed moment of rock'n'roll. There were no tribute bands a generation ago, chiefly because there was no history of rock'n'roll, rock, soul, reggae and pop to deal with in this way. Tribute bands are one aspect of this sense of the history of popular music, and in particular they are part of the demographics of that history – the rock'n'roll generation and its children have grown up with this music, but they are not yet 'old' enough to want to stay at home all the time, and they are happy to replay their youths with tribute bands if the real thing is no longer available, and/or is too expensive, and/or no longer looks the part.

And yet, as is clear from the Brook line-up, at this moment tribute bands exist not just when the band or artist in question is no more, as with T. Rex, Bob Marley, or for that matter the (Bootleg) Beatles, but as often when they are in their prime – thus Green Day and Coldplay also attract this kind of attention. Secondly, therefore, we have to see this kind of music-making as an aspect of contemporary celebrity culture. Celebrity status is a mark of fame, but not of quality or originality. If we apply the notion of popular-media celebrity to music, then, we need a formula something like this: 'music is a commodity delivered not by relatively anonymous, talented, specialised and well-trained musicians, but by the famous, or by people who are prepared to inhabit an aspect of that fame'. While the older tribute bands may deal in an often nostalgic or self-conscious and ironic sense of history, and perhaps appeal chiefly to those who saw the acts the first time round, the current-band tributes are servicing a desire for a symbolic consumption of music and its associated stardom which appeals to those for whom there is little or no absolute value to be found in the 'real' or the 'authentic'.

90 French philosopher Jean Baudrillard coined the word 'simulacrum', meaning a copy which devalued the importance, even the existence, of an 'original'. In the past, he claimed, a cultural phenomenon was literally 'significant' since it was attributed to a single author of the original product, or 'sign'. An individual work of art and its author each had an 'aura' of originality and cultural power. This attitude to present-day tribute bands, a welcoming of the simulacrum which isn't too bothered about the authority of the original, is part of the ease of communication to be found in the digital era: *the sign itself has indeed lost its aura,* and the reproduction of the sign has therefore gained in status as well as in enjoyability.

But there's a contradictory impulse, as usual, in copyright law as applied to public performance – which still insists on the authority of an original. A third aspect of the tribute band is its effect on musicians and musicianship. Local musicians (and occasionally far more than that, as with the leading Abba tribute of the 1990s, the Australian band Bjorn Again) find that they can only get a booking, let alone make a living, when playing other people's music. This implies that there is no room for creativity and originality in rock and pop outside the demographic envelope (under 25) in which new acts can be seen as a promising 'unsigned' singer or band; or of course if/when they are signed, or otherwise make their way to chart and/or touring success, with original compositions which might earn some of them a reasonable livelihood. But for the tribute band there is a key constraint on that livelihood: tribute bands will have to exist on performance fees alone, while the venues and management will have to pay composition royalties to the composers and other copyright holders associated with the various bands to which they pay tribute.

The tribute band is a global phenomenon which flourishes outside the Anglophone world – take for example the phenomenon of the Genesis tribute. The Genesis Tribute website lists bands based in the USA, the UK, Brazil, Canada, the Czech Republic, Denmark, Germany, Italy, and the Netherlands, while two Norwegians offered recitals of the band's music arranged for two pianos, and three Brits played arrangements for classical guitar trio. Most of the tributes concentrate on material which Genesis themselves no longer perform. Among the most exact of these tribute bands, Canada-based ensemble The Musical Box, offers a facsimile of Genesis' highly theatrical performances from

1973–5, with simulated costumes, lighting design and choreography as well as exact copies of the music from albums such as *The Lamb Lies Down on Broadway* (1974) performed using original instruments.

Historicisation has also been applied to black music in the USA, the UK and elsewhere – though black artists have always had to work within significantly different historic and contemporary conditions of production and consumption. Apart from the great success story of Tamla Motown in the 1960s, and latterly of a few hip-hop artists and the labels associated with them such as Death Row Records, much of the money invested in black music has been by white-owned corporations. The result has been a perception of under-investment in artists' careers; star performers therefore rise and fall in a different pattern, and their historic celebration is different. But much of American jazz since the 1960s, and most of early hip-hop, are themselves manifestations of a historic awareness, as the artists involved imitate and rearrange, sample, remix and replay the legacy of black American music. This is at the same time history, cultural preservation, and renewal.

Meanwhile rapping itself – speaking or chanting rhymes over beats – has become an ordinary part of almost all popular music, present in for example nu-metal, pop, and dance music alike, and in each case it has taken the music in a number of different and innovative directions, helping to renew rather than just recycle or preserve. For cultural critic Paul Gilroy, the result is often a musical hybridity which signifies an open and honest account of the important place of black culture within the Western world. Gilroy has celebrated the Streets – a.k.a. their (white) composer and vocalist Mike Skinner – as an example of this new hybridity, which acknowledges and celebrates an open multiethnic multiculture of the urban world. Similar points might be made about white bands whose music is at one remove from the half-spoken delivery of Mike Skinner; say, the Arctic Monkeys' songs, which represent the new urban realism with gentle humour, or even Franz Ferdinand's witty pop-rock.

Acts such as the Arctic Monkeys and Franz Ferdinand seem at the same time to belong to the old world and the new: in each case internet-based marketing strategies helped them to achieve decent-sized fanbases; but the bands themselves consist of youngish people, playing oldish-sounding music which is 'indie' in attitude, relatively rough in sound values, and with lyrics which are witty, brief and to the point. The Streets, Franz Ferdinand, the Arctic Monkeys, and their immediate successors are in one sense the latest inheritors of the music-hall-to-Pulp tradition of songs with witty words which go beyond the staple of romantic love. They, just like the tribute bands, are part of the remaking of musical history. But unlike the tribute bands these are indeed oldish-sounding rather than merely copies of the old: they are not merely stuck in a musical groove from the 1900s, the 1960s or any other point in the past.

Those witty words might be rapped or recited as much as sung, indicating once again the importance of hip-hop to all popular music since 1980, and perhaps also indicating that this phenomenon of white rap is the latest example of the 'phantom dialogue' in indie pop/rock. So here are the opposite of the present-day tribute bands: in this sense originality and authenticity are not dead, and we have here not a simulation, but a living and evolving tradition.

In some ways what is happening here might be a surprising phenomenon: through historicisation and hybridisation alike, we can see the strategic survival of rock in the age of dance music. Through rapping to turntablists, riffing guitarists or both, the sonic world of rock has been renewed, when towards the end of the 1980s many people thought that bedroom-made electronica, lined up and sequenced by DJs, would simply relegate it to history. We should not be surprised. Almost since the start of rock'n'roll pundits have been predicting the 'death of rock', and yet it has consistently and obstinately refused to die. Phenomena such as grunge, the continuing underground presence of hardcore punk (leading to the mid-2000s mainstreaming of 'emo' as well as the success of Green Day), and the impact of nu-metal, have kept various sub-genres of rock alive and well, thus also making space for the continuing arrival and development of rock orthodoxy in world-selling bands like Coldplay.

The historical framing of dance music

The survival of rock in the age of dance is doubtless cause for celebration. But we should also celebrate the survival of dance music itself. This book was scheduled for publication in the summer of 2007, nineteen years after the 'second summer of love' saw the illegal outdoor parties of London's M25 greenbelt, the warehouse parties of Lancashire, and the brief incarnation of 'Madchester' as a globally hip city. In other words, some of the 18–19 year olds, students perhaps, reading fresh copies of this book will have been the issue of romantic liaisons which started at legal or illegal parties or dance clubs in the late 1980s. At that point, the new music and its associated mix of drugs and parties might have felt, to their parents, like a brief subcultural moment, which would be gone within three years or so; in fact similar music is still being made, and danced to by young people. Dance music, too, is a survivor.

Aspects of the then new dance culture were explored in some of the best-selling novels of the 1990s: among them Irvine Welsh's *Trainspotting*, his collection of short stories *The Acid House*, and Hanif Kureishi's novel *The Black Album*. But perhaps the strongest gauge of the strength of the continuity of this experience within UK popular culture is its presence in a decade of feature films: among these are *Trainspotting* (based on Welsh's novel, and directed by Danny Boyle in 1996), *Twin Town* (directed by Kevin Allen, 1997), *Human Traffic* (directed by Justin Kerrigan, 1999), *Sorted* (directed by Alexander Jovy,

2000), *South West 9* (directed by Richard Perry, 2001), and *It's All Gone Pete Tong* (directed by Michael Dowse, 2004). While these are all very ambivalent texts – each can be read as a morality tale about the dangers of excessive drug use, though each has also been accused of glorifying the experience – they are an important register of the quotidian normality of the association of dance music parties and drug use among the young, and of the continuing association between party culture, drug use and popular music: each has an associated soundtrack album.

93

There was also a very strong journalistic and academic interest in the new dance culture. The literature of the dance decade also survives in relatively good shape through publications such as *Mixmag*, which was started in the late 1980s as an indie magazine, and its US sister publication, *Mixer*; the independent *Dazed and Confused*, founded in 1992, owing its title to a track on the first (1969) album by Led Zeppelin, but very much on the button of the Madchester/Dance scenes; and *The Wire*, which when founded in the late 1980s was celebrating yet another short-lived 'revival' of British jazz, but by the late 1990s had recognized the pioneering force of the new electronica, and was trying to find the artists within the genre whose work best represented the magazine's tendency to valorise whatever produces the most uneasy listening.

The new magazines of the late 1980s had been necessary because when Acid House took off in the late 1980s the British music press remained resolutely rock-centred, supporting the white-boy guitar bands which were to emerge from the 'indie' sector into the mainstream in the Britpop era. But one of its more intelligent writers changed the terms of rock criticism from self-righteous analysis to self-dissolving appreciation, grasping remembered moments of epiphany which reflect those celebrated by most of the writers on dance music. Columnist Simon Reynolds insisted in his first book, *Blissed Out: The Raptures of Rock* (1990) that rock music at its best actually *bestows* a lack of control on the listener, enabling him or her to escape from the socially constructed education–work repressions of everyday subjectivity. At this point he responded coldly to the new acid house. Eight years later, in the 1998 book *Energy Flash, A Journey Through Rave Music and Dance Culture*, Reynolds reverted to the adoration he had expressed in *Blissed Out*, but with dance music as his new musical object of desire.

The argument running throughout *Energy Flash* is that the more basic and repetitive the music, and the more it confers on dance participants that state of release from routine mental operations Reynolds dignifies with the term 'bliss', the better. Repeated rhythm leads to the disappearance of the ego – though the highest ecstasy of disappearance, in the utopian moments of Reynolds' and many similar accounts, is related to the first disappearance of an Ecstasy tablet down the throat of the participant. There follows an experience in which, in Reynolds' words, 'the Dionysian paroxysm' seems to the willing participant as if it has been both achieved and 'programmed and looped for eternity'.[21]

Of course it wasn't, and isn't. The world continues to turn even while parties are in full swing, and as dance events come to an end, most of the participants – however much they have achieved a state of fluid, depersonalised amorphousness on the dance floor – remember who they are, resolve into individual human beings once more, return to school, university, or the office, and continue to play their parts in the current system of production, distribution, exchange and consumption – of which the production, distribution, exchange and consumption of dance music and Ecstasy are component parts. Matthew Collin, in one of the most careful of the late-1990s journalistic accounts of the dance era, noted that economic forecasters The Henley Centre claimed in 1993 that the dance scene in Britain was worth £1.8 billion annually, about the same as book publishing; in 1996 the British Tourist Board's attempts to recruit younger visitors to Britain focused on the provision of clubs and rock music; the gradual rise to hegemony of the club 'brand' is one result.[22] The official licensing of 'superclubs' such as Cream and the Ministry of Sound in the early 1990s has led to the formation of global brands involved in the provision of a range of leisure services and retail products such as the clubs themselves; open-air day parties and longer festivals such as Creamfields; branded leisure clothing; compilation CD and DVD albums; and 3G audio and video streams for mobile phones.

Perhaps the most important official response to the Acid House phenomenon occurred in relation to the use of alcohol. In the three years following the large-scale arrival in the UK of Ecstasy, alcohol sales in public houses fell by some 20 per cent: young people using Ecstasy apparently preferred to drink water. In a repeat of the 1960s counter-counter-cultural moment in which cannabis use was more strictly controlled despite positive official advice about its use and effects, Ecstasy was classified as a Class A drug, and simultaneously, thanks to the fierce lobbying of the alcohol industry, alcoholic drinks were reinvented to make the legal drug more appealing to the young. During the key year 1995 a single Ecstasy-related death was used to drive a mass-media campaign against the use of the drug, while the government sanctioned the televised advertising of spirits for the first time, and a number of ads which represented gin, vodka and rum as young people's drinks followed. Even more subversively, 1995 also

---

[21] Simon Reynolds, *Energy Flash. A Journey through Rave Music and Dance Culture* (Picador 1998) p.xvi

[22] Matthew Collin with John Godfrey, *Altered State: the Story of Ecstasy Culture and Acid House* (Serpent's Tail 1997) pp.267–71

saw the introduction of 'alcopops', drinks which mixed spirits with sweet flavours such as lemonade or blackcurrant. These products appeared to have been engineered to entice underage drinkers, especially young women, to become regular users of alcohol.

Furthermore, 1995 was also the key year of Britpop, an important moment in the recycling of past musics. While Blur and Oasis stormed the singles and album charts in a flurry of laddish aggression, nostalgia and whimsy, taking their admirers back to the 1960s – including many who were far too young to have been there the first time – the young British public also began to revert to an old drinking habit: using alcohol as a narcotic. The alcoholic strength of alcopops was relatively high by the UK standards of the time, at 5–6 per cent by volume, and the strength of beer rose to meet it. Faced with difficulties of supply and often the relative impurity of illegal drugs, some began to use the legal drug as a narcotic: they drank to become not mildly drunk but completely 'out of it'. The result was not cannabis-induced relaxation, or Ecstasy-inspired feelings of collectively shared emotion, but what alcohol does best: an uninspiring sequence of aggression and anaesthesia. The result of the refusal to decriminalise or legalise class A drugs, coupled with the reinvention of alcohol as a narcotic, gave the average UK town centre a strange new look on a weekend evening: young people went 'binge drinking' – consuming very large quantities of alcohol. The results included massive increases in male-on-male and female-on-female violence, and in allegations of 'date rape' in which the victim was so drunk as to be virtually senseless at the time of the assault. While the Ministry of Sound website links to a great deal of non-judgmental information about illegal drugs, in November 2005 the original Ministry of Sound building in South London, which had been refurbished complete with cocktail bars, was awarded a 24-hour drinks licence, so its customers could now binge to the beat without thought of tomorrow. Even in the dance music which Reynolds celebrated in 1998 as the ultimate music of 'resistance' there is no necessary connection to the end of the commodity–capitalist world as we know it today. The dance revolution has been recycled and remade into club culture; and club culture is big business. Like classical music, dance music had become pop.

Chapter five

Business strategy and cultural policy in the digital era

Most of the developments discussed so far have been aided and abetted by digitisation, which has undoubtedly meant that more music is available to more people more of the time. However, this is not a world structured through free and open choice, but by legal constraints which are vital to the functioning of the music business. This chapter complements the previous two by exploring the ways in which the music business has responded to the age of abundance.

Music, business and the law

In many parts of the world in the last quarter of the twentieth century the music business, though successful by any standards, lobbied governments for further legal and financial support. One result was a 'blank tape levy', imposed on the purchasers of recordable media. Though this tax was, it was argued, to compensate the industry for consumers' copying of materials they had bought, at the same time, and again thanks to record business lobbying, a serial copy management system or SCMS was built into the hardware of consumer devices such as digital audio tape (DAT), CD and minidisc recorders. The SCMS effectively prevented users from making more than one digital recording of any commercial disc.

In the first five years of the new century the global recording industry, which had fiercely lobbied governments for extended copyright privileges, took action against the owners and software writers of P2P file-sharing programmes such as Napster and Kazaa, which allowed users to access and copy from each others' collections of digitally encoded music files stored on their own computers' hard drives. The Recording Industry Association of America (RIAA), and the British Phonograph Industry (BPI), subsequently began to take legal action against individual users of swapped MP3 files – including a few notorious examples where parents were prosecuted and fined for the activities of children as young as twelve.

Elsewhere in the music business an attempt to control consumers' use of music they had actually paid for backfired badly when in late 2005 users reported damage to their PCs. Sony BMG had marketed a number of CDs, by artists including Britney Spears and Foo Fighters, which contained sophisticated copyright protection systems in order to enforce what the industry referred to as Digital Rights Management (DRM). As well as preventing the user from making multiple copies, these programmes contained hidden spyware devices which remained in a user's computer and could disable that computer's CD drive. After a number of public legal proceedings in New York, Texas and California, Sony BMG was forced to offer compensation to people who had bought these CDs, as well as withdrawing the CDs themselves from the market.

Such hostility against consumers – the Sony spyware was after all intended to infect legal purchasers' computers – was all the harder to understand because copyright law was already working in the industry's favour. The most important act in the reformation of international copyright law was the passage of the Digital Millennium Copyright Act (DMCA), which was signed into American law by President Bill Clinton in 1998, and subsequently became the model for legislation elsewhere, such as the UK Copyright and Related Rights Regulations of 2003. The DMCA prohibited consumers from circumventing manufacturers' copy-protection systems, thus formally denying their right to copy from materials they had legally purchased. It gave internet service providers (ISPs) limited liability in relation to copyright infringements taking place within their domains (as long as they control them when ordered to do so). While the DMCA did not specify P2P file-sharing as an offence (because the problem did not in fact emerge until 1999), crucially, it gave the entertainment industry the right to obtain from ISPs details of companies and individuals who were engaged in copyright infringements. Thus the campaign against Napster included a notable PR stunt, which was pulled on 3 May 2000, when a list of 335,435 names of alleged illegal downloaders of music by the band Metallica was delivered to the Napster headquarters by truck.

Less visibly but perhaps more importantly, one in fifty of all lawsuits in the USA in 2005 was brought by the music business against one or more alleged illegal downloaders, and/or their parents: in other words, quite apart from the extreme activities of Sony BMG in its DRM war on people who had actually bought its products, the music business was spending a great deal of time and money suing its actual or potential customers. Such interventions against individuals, whether or not they are facilitated by the DMCA, raise serious issues of data protection and individual human rights which have been only partially tested at the time of writing in a number of ongoing cases.

It is worth emphasising at this point that – as the mention of human rights implies – there is indeed an *ethical* debate about music and its ownership and uses which is at least as important as the entertainment-industry-driven *legal* concern over the maintenance and enforcement of their copyright. There are a number of issues here including the right of the originators and/or performers of music, including recordings and samples, to be credited by name when their music is reused; and the rights both of consumers and of other musicians to be informed about the sources of the music which they buy and listen to, and might wish to emulate; none of which can *simply* be reduced to a question of ownership, rights and payment.

As importantly what is at stake is the very notion of the existence of a culture held in common through the exchange of information, whether that be a 'public domain' of cultural materials such as music free for general use, or even a market – a commodified public domain – in which all information, including all cultural material, is generally available for sale. Even this would need a sea change in the attitude of rights owners, who wish to maintain the right to own material that they do not offer for sale. For example, in April 2005 the budget record label Naxos lost a landmark case in the USA in which it stood accused of breaking the law by reissuing some old recordings which were out of copyright. Naxos has reissued a great deal of back-catalogue material by well-known classical musicians from the first half of the twentieth century on CD, usually to reasonably high standards of restoration and transfer. New York's highest court ruled that Naxos had been wrong to release a number of recordings made in the 1930s by the violinist Yehudi Menuhin, even though their copyright had expired and they were not available for sale in any other form outside the USA. The court decided that common law in relation to ownership still covers such recordings. The Capitol label, which had claimed ongoing ownership of the Menuhin recordings in question despite the expiry of copyright, and had offered some of them for sale in the USA only, rightly described the ruling as of 'enormous importance', while Naxos, also rightly, described the ruling as representing 'a certain insanity'. Naxos withdrew several of its re-releases from sale; Capitol did not make the music in question available worldwide. The music business wishes to maintain exclusive rights over catalogues of recorded music, whether or not it wishes to sell the music in question, while pressing for extensions of all and every copyright term; and at the time of writing the American courts, and Congress, have backed it all the way.

99

The digital world offers many new opportunities for business, as for all other ways of creating and exchanging information. However, the Capitol label in this instance, and in most cases the music business more generally, wants a digitalised version of exactly the same sales and production model it has used for fifty years or more, and it has lobbied fiercely, and so far effectively, for such a model to be guaranteed in law. This is another way of dealing with music's history, to go with those outlined in the previous chapter. Capitol's fight for the right to maintain and protect an inaccessible back-catalogue has to do with what it sees as the necessary limits of a market in musical information. If all recorded music were freely available, and there are millions of recordings already in the public domain, why would the music business need to develop new acts and make new recordings? There is already 'enough' recorded music, in the sense that no human being can listen to all of it. The fewer past recordings are available, the more people might be persuaded to buy new recordings.

Indeed, some people might go on to argue, there is very little point in a major label recording, say, yet another version of Beethoven's Fifth Symphony to add to the hundreds which have been recorded so far, many of them played and recorded with exemplary attention to detail, unless only two or three of these versions are available at any one time; and sure enough the major labels' classical catalogues are always in a state of flux, with older recordings being withdrawn (and, often, reissued and repackaged a few years later). The same might be said of albums by, say, jazz piano trios, or blues bands, or female country singers – unless the market is artificially restricted then interest in new recordings, including recordings by new artists, in these genres will be limited; and sure enough CD sales overall are perceived by the music business to have been in decline since the turn of the millennium.

It is precisely at this point that proponents of the new opportunities in digital music-making step in. Music has always been copied; people learn to perform and to write music through listening to others. In effect they learn their own musicality by transforming existing material, and many artists we now think of as truly original started by copying others fairly crudely. An obvious example is the Beatles, who started singing covers of American records, trying to copy them as exactly as possible, and yet within a few years were producing songs of their own which were unlike anything else. Since the advent of hip-hop, however, and in particular since the advent of affordable digital sampling, there has been a step change in the quality of this type of activity, which now involves the use and re-use of existing recordings as well as the copying of rhythms, harmonies and performance styles. Almost all popular music uses samples, and transforms them into something else.

It may seem perfectly legitimate for the owners of copyrights in recordings which are re-used in this way to ask for credit and payment, and for legal disputes to arise when such credits and payments are withheld. In 1985 producer Paul Hardcastle had a hit with a track called '19', an innovative anti-war song which used as its lyrics sampled television news reports from the Vietnam War (the same samples were also very effectively used in the song's video). But '19' also used music samples from the early 1970s blockbuster album *Tubular Bells*, by Mike Oldfield. Virgin, Oldfield's label, sued Hardcastle and won significant damages – they were to be paid a royalty for each copy of the song sold.

This, again, might seem fair enough, though we don't have to look very far to come across far greyer areas in the music business's practice. In early 1987 a throw-together group of musicians called M/A/R/R/S released a single called

'Pump up the Volume'. The first version did well in the dance clubs, and a remix was also a big hit in the mainstream pop chart. The track was created from drum machine beats, real-time guitar, and samples, and one of the samples featured on the remix was from a song called 'Roadblock', which had been written and recorded by pop producers Stock, Aitken and Waterman (SAW). SAW at first obtained a court injunction to prevent further sales, and sued for damages. The sample was very definitely from a track by SAW, and so in one sense they were quite right to claim legal ownership of and credit for their original work. But 'Roadblock' was not intended to be an 'original' work at all but a *pastiche* – of a mid-1970s soul single – and in that sense it is difficult to sustain the notion of originality or authorship. Nonetheless the SAW lawyers won the day, the track was remixed once again to remove the offending sample, and all overseas sales versions of 'Pump up the Volume' are without 'Roadblock'.

The 'cultural and creative industries'; the problem of media literacy

So the law has often upheld the rights of the owners of copyright. The music business has in turn lobbied government for further protection, and in doing so it has stressed the importance of music as one of the strongest of the 'creative and cultural industries', which are claimed to be vital to future economic development in parts of the world which no longer have large-scale industrial production – such as the UK.

The New Labour government came into power in the UK in 1997 on a wave of popular optimism partly fuelled by the positive recent story of pop – the local impact of Britpop and the global success of the Spice Girls. Among the first acts of the new government was to recreate and rename the old Department for National Heritage, which had looked after museums and art galleries, historic buildings and archaeological sites: it became the Department for Culture, Media and Sport (DCMS). As the title implies, the new ministry was given a very wide brief – but its overall focus was to strengthen the contribution of all these areas of life to the development of the national economy. In the words of the new Government's 1997 election manifesto, 'Art, sport and leisure industries are vital to our quality of life and the renewal of our economy. They are significant earners for Britain. They employ hundreds of thousands of people. They bring millions of tourists to Britain every year.'[23]

Thus the new government announced its support for 'the creative industries'.

---

[23] The Labour Party's 1997 manifesto, *New Labour Because Britain Deserves Better,* is available unpaginated but in full at www.psr.keele.ac.uk, which was accessed 8 December 2006.

New Labour saw them simultaneously as a sign of modernity; an export earner; and a provider of work in which people from disadvantaged areas and disadvantaged social and ethnic groups might actually be interested. Thus apparently a thriving 'creative economy' would provide social inclusion, widening participation and economic regeneration all on the one ticket. The Department for Culture, Media and Sport produced an audit of these activities, a 'creative industries mapping document', which first appeared in 1998 and was updated in 2001. Through a raft of policies such as the New Deal for musicians (which was a form of enhanced social benefit payment for people learning to be popular musicians), reviews of the financing of musical enterprises, and a requirement for all local authorities to produce culture-for-inclusion policies of their own, the new government attempted to reinforce the message that promoting culture and creativity were viable ways of modernising society and economy alike.

In response to this agenda even the principal distributor of subsidies from government coffers to professional high-culture performers, writers and artists, Arts Council England, reinvented itself, in part, as an agency aiming for the promotion of social inclusion and the celebration of diversity – and it was rewarded with significantly increased overall funding. Arts Council England's strategy document for 2003–6, for example, seemed to be an open-access policy, continually emphasising that 'the arts' are for everyone, and claiming optimistically that artistic events can simultaneously and magically help to transform communities, celebrate cultural diversity, and maintain a tradition of rewarding excellence. But on closer reading the document makes some more interesting points, as here, where the routine access-speak is juxtaposed against a growing anxiety, indeed a very real fear of the impossibility of genuine communication in an era of information overload:

> We believe that access to the arts goes hand in hand with artistic excellence. Participation, contribution and engagement in the arts are the bridge between access and excellence. That bridge is especially crucial in a society which is itself subject to ongoing change: more culturally and ethnically diverse; more educated and informed but also more distracted and cacophonous.[24]

This fear is echoed in many parts of the world as the growth of information continues to exceed the human capacity to decode it all: in the bleak logic of this view, too much cultural information simply becomes noise; cultural overproduction is just like any other.

---

[24] www.artscouncil.org.uk/aboutus/ambition.php, accessed 16 September 2006

In order to combat this knowledge gap in the digital age, a particular kind of education is of growing importance. The utopian vision of techno-lifestyle-choice is offset by the industry's huge fears about originality, piracy and theft, but also by these equally fundamental fears about the capacity of the population to make such choices in an informed way. The proliferation of new communications technologies has brought with it a new form of anxiety within the entertainment industry about the ordinary user's lack of media literacy, which the industry has begun to see as a key inhibitor of take-up. As a result it is beginning to promote 'media literacy' as an aspect of education.

103

However, there's often a mismatch between educational and business expectations of the nature of media literacy education. As far back as 1982 UNESCO declared that 'We must prepare young people for living in a world of powerful images, words and sounds'. At around that time the Center for Media Literacy was set up in the USA in order to promote education in media literacy at all levels (though it concentrates on secondary school education). The Center's work promotes the concept of informed enquiry, in which students are taught how to access information, analyse and explore how the media's messages are constructed, evaluate those messages against the student's own beliefs and ethical principles, and express and/or create their own messages using a variety of media tools. Texas has included this type of media literacy as a standard part of the school curriculum. Similar initiatives exist in Australia, Canada and France, and in the UK, including academic Media Studies at school and university. Media Studies often takes a sociological approach to the study of media messages, and this usually left-oriented discipline therefore tends to be highly critical of the ways in which the dominant media corporations encode, distribute and sell their material.

A critical – and often openly hostile – approach to the media's messages is not precisely what the entertainments industry itself means by 'media literacy'. Yes, the industry argues, education must empower users to access and understand messages, but it must also empower them actually to use the equipment which delivers the messages. The industry fears that everyone else feels inhibited or alienated by technological complexities and inter-operability problems. The advertising copy accompanying the Arcam thirtysomethings image referred to in chapter three raises this issue, which has become increasingly common in the digital age. The brochure's language is predictably, and hyperbolically, technical, but the anxiety over the user's ability to navigate in the range of choices involved is clear:

> The DV79 uses parts and techniques more commonly seen in sophisticated specialist broadcasting equipment to great effect. The audio engineering, as you would expect from Arcam, is also state of the art. The player comes with all the video and audio outputs you could possibly need and, as well as

playback of regular DVD-Video discs and CDs it will also, unlike many well-known machines, handle CD-R and CD-RW discs plus HDCD and most MP3 encoded CDs.[25]

The equipment has the ability to decode information from a bewildering range of sources; in order to derive maximum benefit from this expensive equipment, then, the user must achieve some expertise in those sources and the ways in which they encode music, and the very different ways in which their indexing software is addressed by the Arcam device itself.

In order to address this literacy deficit the broadcasting and music industries have campaigned for potential consumers to be given the technical skills to use the products they are trying to sell. Broadcasters in the UK began to campaign for wider literacy skills in the late 1990s, and the DCMS backed this approach. The DCMS-supported campaign resulted in *The Charter for Media Literacy*, which was launched at the British Film Institute on 10 November 2005 by then junior culture minister James Purnell MP. His speech included the following:

> The media provide us with distinctive and vital means of expression; are a dominant and global source of information, stories and opinions; and form an important part of our cultural heritage. If people are to participate fully and effectively in today's world, they now need to be literate in all forms of media. We are committed to:
> * Raising public understanding and awareness of media literacy, in relation to the media of communication, information and expression;
> * Advocating the importance of media literacy in the development of educational, cultural, political, social and economic policy;
> * Supporting the principle that every UK citizen of any age should have opportunities, in both formal and informal education, to develop the skills and knowledge necessary to increase their enjoyment, understanding and exploration of the media.[26]

The UK organisation charged with the regulation of the broadcast media, Ofcom, meanwhile, was charged by government with improving media literacy. In order to do this Ofcom surveyed the use and take-up of new media products in the UK population.[27] It reported early in 2006 that mobile phones were in ubiquitous use among all age groups. Younger people had taken to the enhanced functionality of mobile phones, whilst for older users they remained predominantly communications tools. However, they reported that use of the

---

[25] www.arcam.co.uk, accessed 28 November 2006

[26] www.ukfilmcouncil.org.uk/information/downloads/, accessed 16 November 2006

[27] www.ofcom.org.uk/research/tce/report/, accessed 21 November 2006

mobile as a 'memory device' to look back at stored texts and pictures is commonplace for all age groups.

While the use of music was not part of the survey's parameters (which is itself an interesting omission), Ofcom's survey provided some interesting and worrying information about the place of music in the national imaginary. Predictably enough among the proliferation of platforms and opportunities for media engagement, television's place was being challenged by the internet, and among under-24s by the mobile phone; but whatever their chosen platform for communication and access to information and entertainment, the place of music in the public affection seemed to be diminishing. A large majority of those surveyed – 71 per cent – still listened to music at home on a hi-fi, while 18 per cent admitted to regularly listening to music on an MP3 player or other portable device. However, while there was much reliance on television and on the internet among the under-50s, only 13 per cent of those surveyed said that of all their media consumption they would miss listening to music at home the most, and only two per cent said they would miss their music portable devices more than anything else.

105

This evidence would seem to challenge the popular notion of a music-hungry younger generation eager to beg, borrow or steal every scrap of musical information available. Games, which are both audio-visual and interactive, are quite simply more important to the young than the relatively passive receipt of commercial music. However, when discussing the personalised preferences expressed by young people in their uses of new technology, Ofcom reported that one third of 12–15 year olds have direct experience of creating ringtones and playlists, while around half have either experience of or interest in setting up their own website and making a short film using a digital camcorder. Once again we note that, while music has a relatively subordinate place in this list of activities, both ringtones and playlists are key aspects of musical choices and activities in the digital age. Facility with ringtones, as listed here, includes the making of new ringtones – this is a very crude form of composition – as well as the downloading (and swapping and sharing via Bluetooth) of commercially available ringtones. Playlisting, whether on computers or phones, involves the selection and organising of musical favourites; challenging the aura of 'the album'.

However, in the end the Ofcom survey is gloomy news for those who believe in the importance of maintaining the cultural importance of music. The survey indicates that music is relatively unimportant to most children, with only 13 per cent of those aged 8–11 and (perhaps especially disappointingly) only 27 per cent of those aged 12–15 identifying listening to music on a portable MP3 player or similar device as a priority; while a little more positively nearly half of 12–15s identified listening to the radio as a prime activity. All are far more likely to watch television, surf the internet and/or use a mobile phone regularly, and all identified television, the internet and the mobile phone as the media resources they value most highly and would find it most difficult to do without.

Of course television, the internet and mobile phones are all carriers of a great deal of music; early research into the impact of 3G phones in Japan contradicted the Ofcom findings, suggesting that music, not video-based material such as television, was the most widely downloaded content. Nonetheless the impression remains that in the digital cornucopia music, of itself, is just part of the general noise of information overload (what that Arts Council strategy document referred to as the 'distracted and cacophonous' aspect of contemporary society), and music is therefore of decreasing importance to the young. If the music industry is to maintain its current level of sales, let alone experience growth in the future, then media literacy strategies will need to evolve to take this into account. At the time of writing the mobile phone industry was still debating ways in which to promote increased take-up of 3G services, with much anxiety expressed at the annual 3GSM trade festival in Barcelona in February 2007.

Chapter six

Reflections on the future of music

M/A/R/R/S's 'Pump up the Volume' was a landmark record musically as well as legally. Removing one sample from one clever song could not remove the technique that had put it there in the first place, which now entered the general musical consciousness. In these late 1980s days of Acid House a number of musicians made innovative use of samples of all sorts and from any source – collaging and sequencing extracts from radio broadcasts, television (especially children's television), official information film and newsreel, as well as from music recordings. Artists approached the new technologies with a sense of playful fun. Among the chart hits of the time were 'Bass: How Low Can You Go' by Bomb the Bass, and 'Doctorin' the House' by Coldcut, with feature vocals by Yazz, who went on to have a brief career as British House music's first star singer with 'The Only Way is Up!' Whether they meant to or not, M/A/R/R/S had helped to change popular music.

The result was a new vocabulary of musical creativity to go along with the new techniques: people talked about breakbeats and loops, layers and sequences. Enterprising companies licensed CDs of samples which could then (legally) be used in the formation of new tracks. The original (very expensive) sequencing and sampling devices of the early 1980s were joined by cheaper hardware such as Akai's range of samplers, and as importantly by a number of inexpensive sequencing programmes written for home computers such as the Commodore 64 and the Atari ST.

In a way all this music after M/A/R/R/S had moved music closer to a sense of material held in common, available for reworking by anyone who wished to do so. According to one commentator this type of understanding of musical material had always been around the corner. Consider the prophecies made by Jaques Attali in his influential 1978 book *Noise*. The gramophone, Attali argued, had been developed to preserve sounds; but it ended by replicating them. Repetition, and the ability to replicate sounds faultlessly even in live performance, then became the ultimate musical value, the norm against which everything was judged.

This vision of conformity seems to apply to all post-1988 dance music and the cultures surrounding it. It may therefore look a little bleak. Yet at the same time, Attali foresaw, the ways in which repetitive music was constructed would bestow an exit from this increasingly meaningless world. Technology, he argued, would become a means of escape from mere repetition, ushering an era in which all of us can become composers. Experimental composer John Cage's work in the 1950s, for example, prefigures the reintroduction of the sounds of the street; sure enough, a generation later samplers make routine the incorporation of such noises into music, and Public Enemy's records are as likely to feature police sirens as funky drumbeats. Indeed, the new instruments foreshadow a new epoch. Composing as a differentiated function will disappear, claimed Attali. People will create their own compositions, into which images are incorporated rather than the reverse, while in the new composition 'rules dissolve'. And rules have indeed, dissolved in the last twenty years, as American computers, German and American composing software and Japanese record decks and high-technology instruments have enabled people without traditional musical skills to become composers. Writing in 1978, before the era of the personal computer, Attali prophesied both the invention of software such as Apple's *GarageBand* and *Soundtrack* programmes, and the set of cultural social attitudes to music which go along with them.

These attitudes challenge principles which are still taken for granted elsewhere, for example in music education as well as in the music business. In both *GarageBand* and *Soundtrack*, the user is invited to compose a new track by arranging loops of existing material in sequences and layers. In the words of the manual for *Soundtrack*:

> Now, using digital music tools and applications, video editors, including those with no musical training or experience, can create high-quality soundtracks for their video projects with the same personal computer used to assemble and edit their video. Using Soundtrack, even non-musicians can create professional-sounding, royalty-free soundtracks… and create original musical compositions. Soundtrack lets you build musical arrangements using pre-recorded audio files called *loops* and *one-shots*. Loops contain rhythmic patterns that you can extend to fill any amount of time, while one-shots contain sound effects and other non-repeating audio. You combine and arrange loops and one-shots in the Soundtrack timeline, add professional-quality effects, mix your music in stereo, and export the final mix to a standard audio file that can be played on any multimedia-equipped computer.[28]

Once you have chosen a 'project key', any loops or one-shots you load in will automatically be set to play in that key, so you don't need to spend any time learning about the rules of tonal harmony. *Soundtrack* includes the facility for the user to record their own audio material, whether vocal or instrumental,

---

[28] *Soundtrack Pro user's manual*, Apple Inc., Cupertino, CA, 2003, p.9

though it does not include the MIDI interface for the use of external devices such as synthesisers or samplers, or the score-writing subroutines, which are a normal part of most computer-based composition packages. But this real-time performance, whether or not it is then edited, is an entirely optional extra rather than the centre of the musical process.

Many users of these programmes on Apple computers will be video professionals looking for a quick way to finish a product on which they have worked hard to produce original visual material. But the same attitude to music composition is equally clear from the 2006 instruction booklet for a popular Sony Ericsson mobile phone which has no obvious professional application:

109

> Compose and edit your own melodies to use as ringtones. A melody consists of four types of tracks – Drums, Basses, Chords and Accents. A track contains a number of music blocks... of pre-arranged sounds with different characteristics. The blocks are arranged into Intro, Verse, Chorus and Break. You compose a melody by adding music blocks to the tracks.[29]

Predictably enough alongside this aesthetic position there are legal and financial considerations. Each of the programmes' manuals make it clear that the existing loops are 'royalty-free', in other words they are not samples of commercially available material for which the user would have to pay a licensing fee. The phone user's booklet contains a warning that 'you are not allowed to exchange copyright protected material', though there seems to be no technological bar on so doing: the phone just gets on with it.

These programmes may be limited in scope, but the message is quite clear: in the digital era, musical composition is principally a matter of cut'n'paste assembly. 'Originality' here lies in the arrangement of existing audio elements; a 'piece' of music is something which is made from quite sizeable chunks of existing material, which use the recorded sounds of instruments and voices to play patterns in genres such as rock, Latin and jazz. The patterns are known as 'blocks' because they can be juxtaposed in any order, or 'loops' because it is assumed that they will be repeated many times. Both *Soundtrack* and *GarageBand*, and the Sony Ericsson phone, offer a form of composition through sample. Musical material is listed; the composer chooses from the list, and then rearranges the chosen blocks. In doing so he or she transforms existing material to create an original work.

Consider the similarities between this approach to music and the archival

---

29 *User Guide W8101,* Sony Ericsson Communications Ltd, Lund, Sweden, 2005, pp.54–5

methods used by MP3 players such as the iPod. These players store digital material which is indexed by multiple identifiers such as track title, album, date and composer; the material can therefore be listed and played in any order, including at random – in 'shuffle' or random play mode an MP3 player can be set to play its entire contents without repetition in any order the player itself chooses – which at the time of writing could mean a maximum of about three months of consecutive eight-hour listening days. New kinds of musicality are available to the listener; new kinds of performance to the user; new kinds of composition to the composer.

The random access approach to musical material maps easily on to the ways in which people represent themselves through what has been called Web2, in public arenas such as www.myspace.com in which the use of personal space often involves the playlisting or cataloguing of musical choices. Though these can be orthodox references to major-label music, they are as often new ways of representing personal taste as a kind of mix. MySpace is often used to publicise users' own music, including the showcasing of unsigned composers, songwriters and bands. Partly as a result in the early 2000s MySpace became one of the last refuges of public enthusiasm for music; many musicians had MySpace pages as well as websites – and this includes well-established artists as well as unsigned bands. Neil Young's 2006 album *Living with War*, for example, was available as medium-quality streaming audio on Young's MySpace site from 28 April 2006, a week before the album's commercial release in CD form. More controversially, also in early 2006, young singer-songwriters Sandi Thom and Lily Allen were being celebrated by the media as 'internet stars' thanks to publicity which had allegedly been generated through exposure on MySpace. There were counter-allegations, that in each case the singer had already signed to a major label, which had funded and helped to produce slick e-marketing campaigns on their behalf.

Web2 pages and playlists might be seen as an innocuous form of presentation through which everyone might achieve their Warholian 15 minutes of fame. But that would not explain why MySpace.com was bought by newspaper and television magnate Rupert Murdoch, owner of Fox, Sky Television, global newspapers such as the (London) *Times* and a great deal of other news and publishing media. Neither would it explain the use of MySpace by established musicians such as Neil Young, who after all have a great many other means of gaining publicity at their disposal. The internet is, increasingly, *primarily* the two-way mirror through which companies can assess our choices and respond through targeted advertising (as Amazon.com already does, inviting the purchaser of goods to buy things its sales system's algorithms claim are similar products). In future, the two-way mirror could monitor the use and payment-per-playback of entertainment forms. *Both the public and the personal, including public and personal space, exist now within a privatised world.*

New musicality for new times

Everything discussed in this book so far has facilitated the development of a new attitude to music which takes for granted the sampler and the MP3 file, and assumes therefore that all existing recorded music is available to be heard but also to be sampled, and, therefore, rearranged and recomposed. We conclude by pondering the changed circumstances of *music* in these conditions which – whatever the changing modes of regulation – have, perhaps fatally, undermined the heretofore existing privileges of the composer and his/her distance from performer and listener alike.

111

Such an approach is increasingly evident from the ways in which music is *thought about*. Since the growth of sampling and the musical uses of the internet there has been a reinvention and republication of work on the conditionality of music; on how we approach it as a historical object (and *whose* past work we value). For example, Michael Nyman's classic text of 1974, *Experimental Music: Cage and Beyond* was reprinted in 1999 in a revised edition with a foreword by the experimental musician and record producer Brian Eno. The same year saw the publication of an important collection of essays edited by Nicholas Cook and Mark Everist, *Rethinking Music*, and in 2003 Les Back and Michael Bull edited *The Auditory Cultures Reader*. Cristoph Cox and Daniel Warner's *Audio Culture: Readings in Modern Music*, another edited collection aimed as much at the general reader as at undergraduates on music degrees, appeared in 2005. Three influential books by regular magazine columnist, experimental musician and cultural optimist David Toop, again written for the general reader, punctuated the decade after 1995. Reading each of these texts one confronts a rejection of the traditional hierarchical power relations of composer-performer-critic-listener, whether they are propagated through elitist avantguardism or rock/pop star systems. In their place is a repeated questioning of what 'music' is now or might be in the immediate future, and a happiness to consider a wide range of possible answers; an attitude prompted in large part by the impact of the new recording and distribution technologies. In other words, these publications – supported by a widening range of academic journals such as *Organised Sound* and general-market magazines like *The Wire* – are beginning to acknowledge that the reconceptualisation of music is an important project.

Re-valuing the musicality of the past: the digital pessimists

Whatever technological and economic changes take place, there is a common assumption that performed and recorded music is, and will still be, vital to our identity. But to some pessimistic commentators the reverse is the case: as they see it the more music becomes generally available, the less important it is to us. Here for instance are the thoughts of Chris Malins, co-founder of the online record collectors' swap shop Vinyl Vulture:

The binary digits that compose the music in its iPod form don't have any value. It's the disposable world of today versus the manufacturing world of yesterday. The analogue culture is very warm and the digital world is very cold and throwaway.[30]

Though this might be read as special pleading from a vinyl record fan – and though we must note that Vinyl Vulture is indeed an *online* concern, and therefore as such part of the digital culture he claims to despise – Chris Malins was not alone in taking this view. Asked to edit an edition of the *Observer* newspaper's monthly music magazine in October 2006, former Pulp lead vocalist and songwriter Jarvis Cocker chaired a discussion entitled 'Does Music Still Matter?' A number of the journalists he talked to claimed that no, music just doesn't mean what it used to, partly because there is so much of it available to so many people so much of the time.

Jarvis Cocker's panellists tended to blame muzak and MP3 players for this state of affairs. For Julian Johnson, defending what he sees as the values inherent in 'classical music', the issue is about the cumulative impact of *all* recorded music:

The absence of… musical debate today suggests a stasis underneath the rapid surface movement in contemporary culture… this in turn suggests a certain lack of concern about music – a sign, perhaps, that music is not as important as it used to be even though it is far more ubiquitous… what doesn't matter to us, we never argue about.[31]

For Johnson, this is the inevitable result of a long historical process in which the key change has been in the changing role of the listener since the invention of sound recording. In the concert hall focused, lengthy concentration was required; but any recording culture 'allows music to function as a thing one possesses rather than a structured temporal event to which one must give oneself up… the CD, the Walkman, and the car stereo tend to flatten out the musical experience', turning all music into part of the background rather than an object of intense contemplation.[32]

Similarly, in January 2006, psychology researchers based at the Universities of Leicester, York and Roehampton claimed that music-buyers were becoming apathetic towards the music they bought or otherwise acquired. 'The

---

[30] Dorian Lynskey, 'Rare Grooves', www.guardian.co.uk, 7 April 2006, accessed 7 April 2006

[31] Julian Johnson, *Who Needs Classical Music? Cultural Choice and Musical Value* (Oxford University Press 2002) p.14

[32] Ibid. pp.53–4

accessibility of music has meant that it is taken for granted and does not require a deep emotional commitment once associated with music appreciation', said the study's co-ordinator, Dr Adrian North. He continued:

> Music can now be seen as a resource rather than merely as a commodity. People might consciously and actively use it in different situations at different levels of engagement, such that listening contexts ultimately determine the value of the musical experience to the individual listener. However the degree of accessibility and choice has arguably led to a rather passive attitude towards music heard in everyday life: The present results indicate that music was rarely the focus of participants' concerns and was instead something that seemed to be taken rather for granted, a product that was to be consumed during the achievement of other goals. In short, our relationship to music in everyday life may well be complex and sophisticated, but it is not necessarily characterised by deep emotional investment.[33]

113

Re-valuing musicality for the present: a digital optimist

The musician and journalist David Toop has made similar points, but from the opposite viewpoint. David Toop has been a musician since the 1960s, producing sounds which owe something to American gurus of experimental modernism John Cage and LaMonte Young. Author of an influential study of hip-hop, *Rap Attack*, Toop produced in *Ocean of Sound* a book which is deliberately not authoritative but suggestive. Twentieth-century music began, he claims, with French composer Claude Debussy's visit to the Paris Exposition of 1889, where he heard a Javanese Gamelan, a village-based ensemble featuring tuned percussion instruments. The Gamelan's music led Debussy away from those narrative structures favoured by Mozart, Beethoven et al. and towards a 'liquid music' which *surrounds* rather than *leads* the listener – which leads Toop to propose the idea that there is a late twentieth/early twenty-first century mode of *hearing*, which is both more and less than *listening*. This aesthetic position values positively what both Johnson and Malins see so negatively. Music, in the age of information overload, simply cannot carry the expressive power of nineteenth-century European concert music and its mid-twentieth-century rock derivatives; so instead it should just be part of the aether, it should float, rather than develop, and we as listeners should literally go with the flow, making chance connections with it as our exposure and concentration levels shift.

This is precisely what Brian Eno has, deliberately and ideologically, tried to do with his 'ambient' music, but such deliberateness is unusual. Toop constantly

---

[33] Charles Arthur, 'Are Downloads Creating Apathy?', www.guardian.co.uk, 12 January 2006, accessed 12 January 2006

makes interesting connections across time and place – but acknowledges that they are the products of his own encyclopaedic knowledge and wide enthusiasm, rather than strategic connections made by other practitioners themselves. A typical micro-narrative occurs when Steve Hillage, lead guitarist of the early 1970s group Gong, and subsequently an ambient dance music pioneer, attends a party where he comes across a DJ who is using a sample taken from one of his records. He introduces himself. The DJ turns out to be Alex Paterson, founder-member of dub/ambient-house band The Orb, who has a record deal with the same label as Hillage – but it turns out that despite the relationship implied by the sample, Paterson knows nothing about either Hillage, or Gong, or any other experimental musicians of the early 1970s, whose music Toop knows to be prophetic of Paterson's own music. (However, whatever the traces of the past might have been, this encounter influenced the future: results of the meeting include Paterson's contributions to the early releases by the ambient dance music ensemble System 7, co-led by Hillage and Miquette Giraudy.)

If musical development can occur through such random events, rather than shared knowledge and deliberate action, does music education, or even a knowledge of the chronological history of music, have any function in the development of 'the creative industries'? David Toop, though he is very knowledgeable himself, might argue that it is neither necessary nor sufficient for succeeding generations of creative people to be aware of the work of their ancestors, as long as they can obtain inspiration from one or other set of sound sources. Alex Paterson, whatever his personal knowledge of musical history, was creatively re-using the music of the past. But from our point of view the necessity for a fully nuanced history of music is, I suspect, increasingly urgent. This is an age where there is more, and more ubiquitous, music than there ever has been. However much we might want to use music as an object of focused contemplation, in practice we all experience music in the way Toop thinks we should do – subliminally, as ambient sound – as we shop, eat, drink, and drive. How are we to differentiate among these experiences, and regain our ability to focus (if we should)?

2004 saw the publication of another Toop journey into sound, *Haunted Weather: Music, Silence and Memory*. Digital technology has changed the ways in which music is perceived, stored, distributed, mediated and created. Writing from what he sees as the cutting edge of these developments, Toop discusses music being made in clubs and exhibition spaces, anywhere and everywhere in the world – much of it on laptops. As he suggests, a single laptop computer 'can be used for recording, processing and composing music, downloading software and sample sounds, editing and mastering an album, burning a CD, designing a cover for the CD, launching a record company with an internet website, making contact with distributors, shops and fans through e-mail, keeping tracks of the company accounts, then taking the computer on the road as a performance tool'.[34] It seems that digital technology has created the preconditions for a new musicality in which we, as either listeners or composers or performers (or indeed all three), can rejoice in the new soundworlds and new modes of communication made available in the digital era.

David Toop is thus ever the optimist. Should he be? His ambient musical dreamworld is precisely what some other critics see as a world which now has *sound* in abundance but is without any genuine *music* at all. In his insistence on the seriousness and importance of music, and on focused listening and performance which underlines this seriousness, this floating, dreaming soundscape is just what Julian Johnson recognises – and rejects:

> Contemporary reception, facilitated by the recorded musical object… implies that music simply exists, that it embraces us in a total, ambient universe, surrounding us at all times and thus dissolving the sense of any one direction or time. The fetish for surround sound and total ambient control of music (turning acoustic space into a kind of amniotic space) aims to make the source of music somehow invisible and, denying its origin in technology, to make it 'natural'.[35]

For Johnson such innovations in the technologies of sound storage and diffusion, far from benefiting music and musicians, are therefore all the more reason that we should work out who owns music, and under what conditions it can or should be reproduced and (re)used.

The discourses of the future

Future 1 – How not to make a freely transformative culture: copyrighting silence

From their rather different viewpoint, the moguls of the music business would tend to agree with Julian Johnson. Indeed, just to prove a point, the major labels and music publishers have even tried to claim the ownership of silence. In September 2002 light music composer Mike Batt (whom we last met as the arranger for Vanessa-Mae, and the talent-spotter who signed Katie Melua to his own label) paid a reported six-figure sum to settle a seemingly bizarre dispute over the copyright ownership of a musical work which consisted entirely of silence. Batt had apparently been accused of plagiarism by Peters Edition, the publishers of the experimental composer John Cage (1912–92),

---

[34] David Toop, *Haunted Weather. Music, Silence and Memory* (Serpent's Tail 2004) p.224

[35] Johnson, *Who Needs Classical Music?*, p.57

after placing a 'silent' track on his band The Planets' first album *Classical Graffiti* (2002). Batt had jointly credited the silent track 13, titled 'a minute's silence', to himself and Cage as composers. There was, he acknowledged, also a rather different musical point to this exercise: track 13 separates a track with a rock accompaniment from a more orthodox ensemble performance by this crossover classical chamber music-meets-rock group. There was also an element of publicity seeking as well as aesthetics in the gesture, as Batt made it known that he had voluntarily paid a royalty to ASCAP, the American Society of Composers, Authors and Publishers, a rights collecting society which operates on behalf of John Cage's recorded work.

John Cage's own silent composition, 4'33", was originally premiered on 29 August 1952. The full score, published in 1952 by Peters Edition, contains three movements, for each of which the solo performer is asked to be completely silent. Cage's intention had been to prove that there could, in fact, be no such thing as a 'silent' piece of music, and sure enough that first performance was accompanied by ambient sounds such as wind and rain, and then after a couple of minutes also by footsteps and doors slamming when angry members of the audience walked out. Cage was pleased with the result.

Peters Edition, noting the joint credit to Cage, asked for a quarter of the composition royalties on the Planets' track. In July 2002, Mike Batt attempted to prove that 'his' silent track differed from Cage's by staging a performance of the piece. He therefore sat in front of a keyboard instrument for a minute. Peters Edition responded by hiring a clarinettist to perform Cage's silent composition in full. Subsequently Batt agreed to pay an undisclosed six-figure sum to the John Cage Trust by way of an 'out-of-court' settlement (though it was never quite clear that the publisher had actually sued Batt). Peters Edition responded to the settlement thus: 'We do feel that the concept of a silent piece – particularly as it was credited by Mr Batt as being co-written by 'Cage' – is a valuable artistic concept in which there is a copyright.' Meanwhile the press had picked up the story, so both Mike Batt and The Planets' debut album had received a great deal of free publicity.

The copyrighting of 'silence' may seem absurd, and if this were just an isolated case which Batt had helped to manufacture in order to gain publicity for his new band, it would be. The problem is that it is by no means isolated. As Lawrence Lessig and Siva Vaidhyanathan have pointed out, and as Joanna Demers argues more fully in her 2006 book *Steal This Music. How Intellectual Property Law Affects Musical Creativity*, the defenders of copyright legislation are continually pushing the boundaries of ownership to include any use of any sonic material in which they have an interest. Notoriously, even the song 'Happy Birthday to You' is subject to copyright control (the catalogue owner at the time of writing was Summy-Birchard Music, a subsidiary of Warner) which theoretically means that its unlicensed performance in restaurants is illegal; on being informed of this some restaurant chains have apparently asked their staff not to perform the song for celebrating clients.

What is happening, argues Demers, is that the music industry is driving the regulation of the new digital technologies in such a way that the creative transformation of existing material – which was vital, for example, in the creative way in which Beethoven responded to and reinvented the music of Mozart, Miles Davis similarly used the music of Charlie Parker, Prince used the music of George Clinton, or for that matter Noel Gallagher of Oasis used the music of the Beatles – is becoming virtually impossible unless the musician involved is already extremely wealthy and has expensive legal backing. In these few cases (such as Puff Daddy, as he was then called, paying a 50 per cent royalty for the use of a Police track on his 1997 single 'I'll be Missing You'), the use of samples can become a form of bling – conspicuous consumption signifying the buyer's wealth above all, just like designer clothing, ostentatious jewellery and fast cars.

Meanwhile for those not already wealthy, sampling and other forms of copying are subject to prohibitively high clearance fees and/or expensive legal action. This means that very few musicians can afford to transform existing musical material in such a way that the listener can recognise it as source material, like, to take a very obvious example, the 1986 Aerosmith/Run DMC collaboration 'Walk This Way'. Every new piece of music would have to be provably original. So unless this was the case the sequences of development and influence we noticed in chapter one, or the covers and tribute bands which were described in chapter six, would be tied in to chains of royalty payment which continue to feed money away from new creation and back to a small number of corporations which have made significant investments in catalogues of compositions and recordings, but need not use the resulting profits to invest in new recordings. The big music corporations are apparently trying to limit licences to a single use, 'pay-per-listen' model. The music industry claims that by protecting its property in this way it is investing in the future of recorded music, and in effect guaranteeing careers for its future creators. Its behaviour would suggest that it is in fact investing far more strongly in the administration of catalogues of existing recorded music, and in paying itself rental income for the right to use the music produced by the ghosts of the musical past.

One commonly agreed result of these legal pressures has been a change in the making of hip-hop. Despite a number of legal disputes in the early days of the genre, for example over the 1979 Sugar Hill Gang track 'Rapper's Delight' (which used not samples, but studio musicians imitating the Chic track 'Good Times'), hip-hop evolved within a framework of acceptable cultural transformation. The concept of 'fair use', which permits authors to use brief attributed quotations from the work of other writers, for example, was thought to apply to musical quotation, whether existing music was imitated through score writing, playing or sampling. Hip-hop artists assumed, in other words, that existing music was there for their fair use, and as a result, as sampling technology developed, recognisable samples of existing materials were almost always the source material for their new tracks. In the 1980s Public Enemy made albums which used hundreds of samples, including speech and sound effects as well as music, and they and their record labels employed lawyers to agree clearance deals for each sample. In some ways the process of clearing has become easier since those early days. Professional copyright 'clearance houses' offer their services, while major labels will usually facilitate enquiries online. EMI, for example, has a dedicated website, emimusicsample.co.uk, through which artists and their agents proposing to use EMI samples can apply for licences to use their chosen material. In offering guidance to would-be samplers, though, the website aggressively makes it clear that the company does not share in any notion of 'fair use'. In their eyes the use of any sample, however short, is potentially litigious:

> UK law prohibits the unauthorised use of the whole of a work or a 'substantial' part of it. Substantiality is both a qualitative and a quantitative test. It is a subjective term. There are common myths that, for example, a use of less than two bars/eight notes/ten seconds does not need clearing. This is not true. There is no 'yard stick'. Laws and practices vary from country to country and evolve constantly. If in any doubt, seek clearance.[36]

Making it relatively easy to clear samples does not necessarily mean making it cheap. By the late 1980s some labels were permitting 'buyouts' – charging fixed payments for the use of a sample, rather than asking the user of the sample for royalties per track sold – but the price for these clearances escalated in turn, from a starting base of around $1,500 per sample to a more usual tens of thousands. In response to these rising costs and the associated legal delays, some artists paid studio musicians to imitate existing tracks, and then sampled the results; others took to using loops from only one song, rather than the tapestry of samples from mainstream Anglo-American recordings which had been used in the 1980s. Subsequently – thanks to cases such as Enigma v. Kuo – even the use of 'exotic' pop, or public domain recordings of traditional music, from the developing world, has become potentially very expensive. As a general rule, the manager of Public Enemy, Walter Leaphard, announced in the early 1990s, the band cannot any longer afford to use samples, since the legal costs involved are so high. The sound of hip-hop has changed notably as a result.

---

[36] www.emimusicsample.co.uk, accessed 12 November 2006

Meanwhile, as Joanna Demers points out, domestic recording technology based around the Mac or PC has become so sophisticated that it is perfectly possible for home musicians both to transform samples beyond recognition, and to make sounds and loops which use entirely original material but sound exactly like recognisable samples. Record label Warner therefore require their artists to keep detailed logs of their use of software procedures in order to be able to 'prove' that the sounds used on their recordings were in fact original.

Future 2 – The qualified utopia of the creative commons   **119**

The apparently reactionary greed of the music and other entertainment companies as they seek to extend the terms of copyright, and their desire to manage all the uses of all their products, has generated a literature of resistance, as well as a great many active resisters. Lawrence Lessig, for example, argues a very clear position in *Free Culture, the Nature and Future of Creativity* (2004). Here's the nub of the argument as Lessig sees it:

> We come from a tradition of 'free culture'... 'free' as in 'free speech', 'free trade', 'free enterprise', 'free will', and 'free elections'. A free culture supports and protects creators and innovators. It does this directly by granting intellectual property rights. But it does so indirectly by limiting the reach of those rights, to guarantee that follow-on creators and innovators remain *as free as possible* from the control of the past. A free culture is not a culture without property, just as a free market is not a market in which everything is free. The opposite of a free culture is a 'permission culture' – a culture in which creators get to create only with the permission of the powerful, or of creators from the past.[37]

Through a number of examples, Lessig demonstrates how in his view 'code becomes law'. Copy-protection software and hardware, euphemistically described as 'digital rights management', has been granted the force of law in the USA by a series of rulings invoking the Digital Millennium Copyright Act. Lessig puts all this in a more general historic context, which is that over the last forty years the entertainment industries have managed to obtain increasing legal protection against copying, file-sharing and commercial or open-source infringements of its software products (recordings), while at the same time extending both the term and scope of copyright, and diminishing the actual rights of the creators they pretend to be defending, including the right of 'fair use'. The end result is that only a very small number of corporations can actually own intellectual property, while the rest of us are obliged to pay them, repeatedly, in return for very limited rights to enjoy what we have paid for.

---

[37] Lawrence Lessig, *Free Culture, the Nature and Future of Creativity* (Penguin 2004) p.xiv

The alternative offered by Lessig is neither a download-utopia free-for-all, nor a cybersocialism of massive state control over corporations in an attempt to guarantee the common good. It is a return to what he believes to be a more genuine free-market capitalism through which the rights of creators and owners of intellectual property can be mutually defended without establishing the tyranny of the past. This is the idea of Creative Commons, a licensing system through which creators can choose to give limited permission for their work to be re-used. The system is designed to harmonise with existing copyright legislation without reproducing its worst aspects. Crucially, it is not big corporations but the creators themselves who can choose the limits – a composer or other copyright holder might choose to limit the duration or number of samples which can be taken from a piece of music, or to encourage educational but not commercial use of the samples.

This kind of limited-use arrangement can (and already does) work very well within a number of digital educational projects. For example, the British Universities Film and Video Council runs a database called EMOL which includes a great deal of digitised material available for educational use. Most of this is film and television, but among their collections is that of former EMI record producer Brian Culverhouse, who has licensed a number of classical music recordings from a career lasting over fifty years. As with existing EMOL collections of film and video, registered users of EMOL can access and use the Culverhouse collection. They are permitted to extract sections of these recordings for delivery either in university virtual learning environments, or on CD. Registered staff and students could download and burn customised CDs, while librarians would be able to replace any that go missing without further payment. In many instances the recordings are accompanied by information about their making, including in some cases marked-up scores used in the actual recordings, which indicate where retakes were needed, or which takes were included in the final release. More of this type of information, including online interviews with original participants, will be added as the collection is developed.

As an annotated repository of musical examples, the Culverhouse Classical Music Collection is already very useful. However, the really innovative aspect of this particular licence agreement is that – very unusually – it allows user manipulation of the sound files, which are available as WAV and MP3 files. Users are permitted to manipulate the WAV files, including stretching or compressing the music in time, looping user-defined sections, and/or altering their pitch. This is indeed a very useful study aid; however, the licence includes all aspects of education, so though there is no licence for any commercial use, film students will be allowed to time-stretch the recordings to fit as soundtracks with their film projects, which may well help to get them jobs in the industry.

Why is all or any of this important? The individual rights of creators are, yes, important, though it does not follow that the owners of catalogues should have exclusive 'rights'. But there's far more to this than a set of legal arguments about existing and future copyright control. Here are some hints:

- 'Postmodernism' as an aesthetic, like the environmental movement's vision of a sustainable ecology, demands that we use and re-use existing materials. Without fair access to the music of the past, future music quite simply cannot be created within this aesthetic.

121

- The proliferation of tribute bands would suggest that signification now works in the absence of an agreed valuation of the 'original'. Digital technologies confirm this – so as we have seen, thanks to the possibility of the perfect digital copy, tribute bands are valued more highly than they were a generation ago when a 'copy' was seen as *necessarily* degraded.[38]

- Computers can manipulate almost any cultural artefact, and this helps many fans to play a part in the reinvention and manipulation of the stories and characters they love. In literature, film and television this kind of interaction is called FanFic or fan fiction ('Slash' fiction in its more extreme, pornographic versions) – there are hundreds of thousands of online stories written by fans, about Harry Potter and friends, the *Lord of the Rings* or *Star Trek* characters, and so on.

- Similarly, the rise of computer games has led many users to generate their own content for the games. They help shape and contribute to the design of the game as well as participating. There's an application on the online Sims game which allows people to download a tool to draw etching round a rug in the living room. A user of the game created this tool, and made it available, free, online; within a few months over four hundred thousand people had downloaded it. Again, multiplayer adventure games such as The Matrix Online are controlled by the actions of the participants, not by an omniscient programmer who decides the outcome of the plot in advance.

---

[38] This point is echoed in the work of the French philosopher Jean Baudrillard, mentioned in chapter four, whose key text *Simulacra and Simulation* was published in translation by the University of Michigan Press, in 1994.

Future 3 – The elements of a 'transformative culture': mash-ups and bastard pop, friendly record companies and the fan remix

Activities of this sort are an increasingly important part of the range of uses of computers in the making and remaking of music, and of a *new musicianship* which is based almost entirely on the re-use of recorded music. Some of those involved in these activities deliberately set out to attack the status quo. Live 'turntablism' involves DJs in real-time collaging, much of which might be technically illegal; but since little of it leads to commercial recordings it is not usually perceived as a major threat by the music industry. More threateningly, John Oswald's project Plunderphonics, and the band Negativland, have made and distributed music using collaged and transformed (but often recognisable) samples from major classical and rock recordings. Their work deliberately challenges assumptions about fair use, and indeed the very concept of copyright itself. Along the way they have collaged music by artists such as Madonna, Michael Jackson and U2 who, they argue, are so rich they do not need extra royalty payments (which might come as welcome news to Michael Jackson). The Plunderphonic and Negativland approach, however, hardly produces 'popular music', in the sense that what they do is not easy to listen to; indeed it is more written about than listened to.

Far more often heard is the equally deliberately subversive use of 'historical' or 'canonic' pop recordings in the subgenre of 'bastard pop', such as the (in)famous *Grey Album*. In 2003 the experimental DJ Danger Mouse (who subsequently became part of the online sales phenomenon Gnarls Barkley) made a combinatory remix – a 'mash-up' – of the Beatles' 1968 *White Album* and Jay-Z's recent *The Black Album*. Jay-Z's album had already been released in a vocals-only version to facilitate the remixes which are so prized within hip-hop and club culture; by contrast, the Beatles' work is notoriously closely controlled, and at the time of writing was not commercially available in MP3 form (the officially sanctioned remix of the Beatles' music, the *Love* album, which was a global hit in December 2006, was sold on CD and DVD-Audio only; the early-2007 agreement between the Beatles and Apple Corp. will probably lead to the band's first official online appearance). Though it was distributed free, the *Grey Album* has been the object of legal action by EMI, the holders of copyright in the *White Album*, but also of widespread internet campaigns and 'download days' such as 'Grey Thursday' in which as many people as possible are invited to swap copies of the *Grey Album* online, a gesture intended to undermine the control of the record labels.

Many acts, like Jay-Z, are now involving their fans at various levels of creativity. In 2004 David Bowie (who, rarely even for a top artist, controls the copyright in all his own work) announced a contest in which his fans were encouraged to submit mash-ups of one piece of his music with any other chosen track. The winner received a very worthwhile prize, a new Audi TT car, but copyright of originals and remixes alike remained in Bowie's hands. More openly, the 2002 Public Enemy album *Revolverlution* features fan remixes of a few old Public Enemy tracks (the album also includes interviews and live performances of older material as well as the remixes, and some new songs). The band's websites had previously made available MP3 mixes of several tracks in either instrumental-only or vocal-only forms, specifically in order for fans to remix them and send in the results. In part this was a deliberate gesture against what this very politically aware band saw as the increasing commercialisation of hip-hop. They continue to encourage fan remixing. In Public Enemy artist Chuck D's words:

> We have a powerful online community through Rapstation.com, PublicEnemy.com, Slamjams.com, and Bringthenoise.com. My thing was just looking at the community and being able to say, 'Can we actually make them involved in the creative process?' Why not see if we can connect all these bedroom and basement studios, and the ocean of producers, and expand the Bomb Squad to a worldwide concept?[39]

They are not alone. In the UK, the XL Recordings label helped in the construction of what it bravely called 'Online Piracy', which was at the time of writing the title of a remix page on British Asian singer MIA's official website. The XL label reasoned that since there were large numbers of unsolicited MIA remixes already online, they might as well join in; the site allows fans to download vocal and instrumental passages from some of MIA's tracks, and upload their own remixes for mutual admiration without fear of reprisal or persecution.

The Real World label also introduced a website for this new kind of fan interaction, realworldremixed.com. They hoped to attract a new audience for their label's acts, encouraging interactive creativity by offering sample packs from two of their best-established artists, Los De Abajo and The Afro Celt Sound System, for remix. Submitted mixes would be put in a chart. The Real World site helpfully listed the software that can be used to prepare remixes, including GarageBand and the similar, loop-based, and free-to-download programme for PCs, Sony's ACID xPress. Dance veterans Coldcut, meanwhile, were offering another kind of fan interaction, their website asking fans to submit videos taken on camera phones during the band's upcoming world tour; again, this material would be uploaded to the website for general sharing, and the best examples would be put on the souvenir DVD of Coldcut's tour.

---

[39] Kembrew McLeod, 'How Copyright Law Changed Hip-hop', www.stayfreemagazine.org, article posted 1 June 2004, accessed 11 August 2006

Given the paranoia about recording expressed by the management and security staff at most venues (it is not uncommon for recording equipment to be confiscated even when it is not in use) this invitation by Coldcut is also in its way an act of deliberate subversion. But – of course – none of this digital engagement with fan communities is pure altruism, and while it is culturally and even legally subversive, it certainly isn't designed to undermine the music business as a capitalist enterprise. As well as promoting interest in the various artists being remixed or recorded, all these interactive websites restrict full access to those who have 'signed up', or in other words provided the label with their personal and contact details. In signing up and submitting remixes, the fan will become part of the online taste-community which services the band or record label. He or she will then be target-marketed with promotional material the artist or record label 'thinks will be of interest' to them. In other words, they will be offered personalised online buying opportunities.

The question might be exactly how 'personal' this is going to get, as the record industry tries to make fans into better customers. In 2001, 5,000 individual digital versions of The Prodigy's song 'Memphis Bells' were sold over the internet in approximately 36 hours. The key word here is 'individual'. Each track sold was not a mere carbon copy, but a variation, a combination of customer-chosen instrumental, rhythmic, and melodic options (of which 39,600 possible choices were available) and in mixes for different sound reproduction set-ups. Five mixes were sold in three file formats, WAV, two audio mixes in MP3, and a 5.1 DTS multichannel audio mix – and all were claimed to be free of any kind of DRM software. Those 5,000 copies were sold in just over 36 hours, in spite of server problems (they tended to collapse due to the demand), which indicates that sales could have been far higher.

However sophisticated (and self-interested) the response of bands and record labels to such phenomena as online remix cultures and fan choice, the continuing significant presence of these interactions confirms the fate of the musical object under digital conditions. Recorded music now has a new utility. Far from being a thing-in-itself, any individual piece of music available in the form of binary digits is now always-already part of a process of transformation, used by the artist and fan alike as an object of re-creation in which originality, even origins themselves, are buried in the semiotic pile of scratch and mix, sample and hold, dub, save and remix. And since each of us, given access to an online computer, can produce and upload our own remix, and/or demand our own bespoke version of a favourite artist's material – we can all 'personalise' a favourite track – in other words, *all music now tends towards the status of the ringtone*. 'You can have any colour you like as long as it's black', Henry Ford's anthem to the efficiencies of mass production, is not an acceptable answer to the digital-era consumer or user of music. We want it our way.

And finally...

It is easy to see that, to the panic of legislators and lobbyists alike, most new music is indeed approaching a state of perpetual copying and/or changing without reference to an original, and that for many users and musicians this has become the cultural norm. As we have seen, the influential French theorist, Jacques Attali, writing in the late 1970s, predicted that evolving music technologies would facilitate a stage whereby everyone composes. Put copying and composition, and put music technologies and communications technologies, together, and we are indeed in the age of Enigma and Gregorian, and also of DJ Danger Mouse and Gnarls Barkley. While the law, still working through long-established notions of authenticity and originality, has so far been successfully invoked to support the rights of Michael Cretu to use and then conceal 'free' source material, but to deny any such rights in existing copyright material to DJ Danger Mouse, the new communications technologies in effect make such a distinction unsustainable.

Music is still, yes, a commodity, increasingly personalised for the individual choice of an aware consumer, and produced by market-savvy musicians and record companies. It is also a source for the re-use of all and sundry with access to a computer. Yet music is also still a form of social cement, bringing people together as musicians and fans alike; and as the recent steps in label–fan interaction prove, increasingly musicians and fans *are* alike; the computer, too, is a social tool even as it cuts and pastes to create new material from old. Therefore music continues to express the fantasy common among politicians that the 'creative industries' *can* somehow at the same time deliver social inclusion, increasing educational attainment, and further economic growth. But in order for this to be possible the music business will have to shed some of its protective attitude, and individual recordings must become less of a commodity and more of a material held in common. We – that is, all those who wish to see music remain as a living and developing entity – need more remix sites, and less copyrighting of silence. The materials of music itself, in other words previous iterations of music in all forms, need to be made freely available, for education; for the transformative use of composers and fans; and for the cultural development of both virtual and real communities.

Glossary

Analogue
The wave-pattern modelling of sound, used in tape recording and in early synthesisers such as the Minimoog.

DAC
Digital-to-Analogue converter. The software which turns the noughts and ones of a digital music file into the pulses which emerge from our loudspeakers as music.

Digital
The modelling of sound using numbers. In synthesisers this means using number patterns to generate sounds themselves. In recording, it means using numbers to replicate a sound event at a particular instant, or sample. The higher the number, i.e. the more times per second, the more accurate the representation of the original sound. See also **Sampler**.

DRM
Digital Rights Management. Software or hardware devices which prevent copying.

iPod
The name of the ubiquitous personal **MP3** player may seem simply right; in fact it rather unromantically stands for *internet Portable Open Database*. The first of these devices, connecting with the owner's PC and, through it, to the iTunes store on the internet, as well as looking maddeningly cool, was offered for sale in November 2001.

MIDI, or the **Musical Instrument Digital Interface**
Agreed by manufacturers of electronic musical instruments in 1981, MIDI is a detailed specification which enables instruments and computers to send performance instructions (pitch, volume, note on and off and so on) to one another either in real time or as stored files. MIDI's importance consists in its global compatibility; it is an open-source protocol, and any MIDI-equipped device by any manufacturer should be able to communicate with any other.

Mobile phone
Launched in the 1980s as an expensive business communication tool, the mobile 'phone' has subsequently dropped in price, become domesticated and ubiquitous even in parts of the world without conventional landline telephones. No longer merely means of talking remotely, mobiles have been developed as a personal storage medium and commercial entertainment device: most manufacturers and service providers currently offer direct connection to commercial music stores both for ringtones and music and video files. The business communications world,

meanwhile, has pioneered more all-encompassing forms of connectivity through the Personal Digital Assistant or **PDA**.

MP3 file
A type of file which compresses music or video files into about a twelfth of their original size – by, to put it simply, stripping out unwanted parts of the original recording such as 'silence'. This makes it far quicker to download and store music and video; without it, the revolution in music use through **iPods** and other personal MP3 players, P2P file-sharing, and the online sale of music and video, would have been highly unlikely. The compression does affect quality, though the user can usually set the amount of compression, and therefore the amount of loss.

Napster
The pioneering peer-to-peer software programme which allowed users to share the music files on each others' hard drives. The Napster company was started in California in 1999, and quickly became a worldwide success. Thanks to a high-profile campaign against music piracy in which star acts like Metallica were backed up by the RIAA's fierce use of the courts, the original Napster was shut down in 2002. The company name survives; Napster now offers a legitimate, music-industry approved service.

P2P, or peer-to-peer file-sharing software
A number of computer programmes which allow the user to access and download information stored on the hard drive of another user's computer. In other words, it facilitated the denial of copyright payment. The most notorious of these programmes was the first version of Napster, a programme which was launched in 1999, and by late 2000 had approximately 80 million users worldwide. After a series of legal interventions by the recording industry, this first version of Napster was closed and a legal programme offering subscription-download of commercial music replaced it; other programmes have since offered the illegal P2P function, and they have also been pursued through the courts.

PDA
Originally very small personal computers capable of synchronising a limited amount of the information on the user's computer, PDAs have become sophisticated mobile phones with enhanced capabilities for synchronising and storing data (including music files), and surfing the World Wide Web.

Playlist
A list of favourite tracks, either in general or for specific purposes. These can be assembled and replayed on an MP3 player or computer; from there they can be shared on dedicated sites or through commercial sales facilities such as Amazon.

Ringtone

A short segment of music which is used in mobile phones as a substitute for the bell-ring of the conventional land-line telephone. In the early twenty-first century the mobile phone's sonic capabilities had increased well beyond the original thin monophonic sounds, and companies started to sell fragments of existing music specifically for use as ringtones. In July 2003 British newspaper the *Guardian* announced that downloaded ringtones had outsold singles in the UK – despite being considerably more expensive.

Sampler

A device which digitally records and stores sounds by 'sampling' them thousands of times per second. The stored sounds can be edited and used in any form of composition in conjunction with a **sequencer**, or played back from any other keyboard or other MIDI-capable device.

Sequencer

A device which digitally records, stores and edits a sequence of musical data which can be either MIDI information or real-time recorded sound or (more usually these days) both. Popular sequencing, recording and editing programmes such as Logic and ProTools have effectively replaced the multi-track tape used in recording studios until the 1990s. Sequencing has therefore become the technical basis of most composition in popular music.

WAV file

A music file which unlike the MP3 stores a great deal of information. As a result the quality tends to be higher.

Bibliography and further reading

John Alderman, *Sonic Boom. Napster, MP3, and the New Pioneers of Music* (Perseus, New York 2001)

Jaques Attali, *Noise*, translated by Brian Massumi (Manchester University Press 1984)

Jean Baudrillard, *Simulacra and Simulation* (University of Michigan Press 1994)

Tara Brabazon, ed., *Liverpool of the South Seas. Perth and its Popular Music* (University of Western Australia Press 2005)

Michael Bull and Les Back, eds, *The Auditory Culture Reader* (Berg, Oxford & NY 2003)

Matthew Collin with John Godfrey, *Altered State: the Story of Ecstasy Culture and Acid House* (Serpent's Tail 1997)

Nick Cook and Mark Everist, eds, *Rethinking Music* (Oxford University Press 1999)

Cristoph Cox and Daniel Warner, *Audio Culture: Readings in Modern Music* (Continuum 2005)

Erik Davis, *TechGnosis. Myth, Magic and Mysticism in the Age of Information* (Serpent's Tail 1998)

Joanna Demers, *Steal This Music. How Intellectual Property Law affects Musical Creativity* (University of Georgia Press, Athens, Georgia 2006)

Tia DeNora, *Music in Everyday Life* (Cambridge University Press 2000)

Kevin H. Dettmar, *Is Rock Music Dead?* (Routledge 2006)

Evan Eisenberg, *The Recording Angel* (2nd edition, Yale University Press, 2005)

Paul Gilroy, *After Empire. Melancholia or Convivial Culture* (Routledge 2004)

Nick Hornby, *High Fidelity* (Gollancz 1995)

Rupa Huq, *Beyond Subculture. Pop, Youth and Identity in a Postcolonial* World (Routledge 2006)

Julian Johnson, *Who Needs Classical Music? Cultural Choice and Musical Value* (Oxford University Press 2002)

Dylan Jones, *iPod, Therefore I Am* (Bloomsbury 2005)

Lawrence Lessig, *Free Culture, the Nature and Future of Creativity* (Penguin 2004)

Ian MacDonald, *Revolution in the Head. The Beatles' Music and the 1960s* (2nd edition, Pimlico 1997)

Richard Middleton, *Studying Popular Music* (Open University Press 1990)

Tony Mitchell, *Global Noise. Rap and Hip-Hop outside the USA* (Wesleyan University Press 2002)

Stuart Nicholson, *Is Jazz Dead?* (Routledge 2006)

Michael Nyman, *Experimental Music: Cage and Beyond* (1974: reprinted 1999)

Simon Reynolds, *Energy Flash. A Journey Through Rave Music and Dance Culture* (Picador 1998)

Timothy D. Taylor, *Strange Sounds. Music, Technology and Culture* (Routledge 2001)

David Toop, *Ocean of Sound. Aether Talk, Ambient Sound and Imaginary Worlds* (Serpent's Tail 1995)

David Toop, *Haunted Weather: Music, Silence and Memory* (Serpent's Tail 2004)

Albin Zak, *The Poetics of Rock. Cutting Tracks, Making Records* (University of California Press 2001)

Index

133